Microsoft Pocket Guide to Microsoft® Internet Explorer 5

PUBLISHED BY
Microsoft Press
A Division of Microsoft Corporation
One Microsoft Way
Redmond, Washington 98052-6399

Library of Congress Cataloging-in-Publication Data
Nelson, Stephen L., 1959-
Microsoft Pocket Guide to Microsoft Internet Explorer 5 / Stephen L. Nelson.
p. cm.
Includes index.
ISBN 1-57231-985-2
1. Microsoft Internet Explorer. 2. Internet (Computer network)
I. Title. II. Title: Pocket Guide to Microsoft Internet Explorer 5. III. Title: Guide to Microsoft Internet Explorer 5. IV. Title: Microsoft Internet Explorer 5.
TK5105.883.M33N454 1999
005.7'13769--dc21

98-45214
CIP

Printed and bound in the United States of America.

3 4 5 6 7 8 9 MLML 4 3 2 1 0 9

Distributed in Canada by ITP Nelson, a division of Thomson Canada Limited.

A CIP catalogue record for this book is available from the British Library.

Microsoft Press books are available through booksellers and distributors worldwide. For further information about international editions, contact your local Microsoft Corporation office or contact Microsoft Press International directly at fax (425) 936-7329. Visit our Web site at mspress.microsoft.com.

Acquisitions Editor: Susanne M. Forderer
Project Editor: Anne Taussig

Microsoft Pocket Guide to Microsoft® Internet Explorer 5

Stephen L. Nelson

Microsoft® Press

The Microsoft Pocket Guide to Microsoft Internet Explorer 5 *is divided into five sections. These sections are designed to help you find the information you need quickly.*

1 Environment

Terms and ideas you'll want to know to get the most out of Microsoft Internet Explorer. All the basic parts of the Internet are shown and explained. The emphasis here is on quick answers, but many topics are cross-referenced so that you can find out more if you want to.

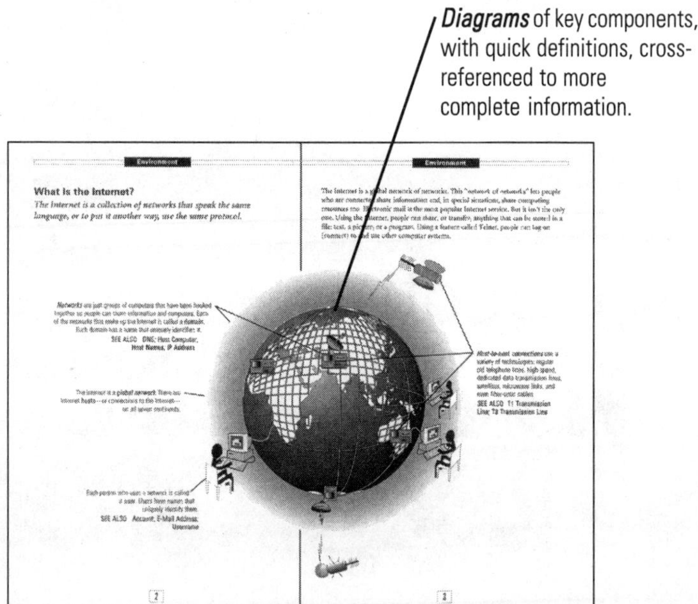

Tips

Watch for these as you use this Pocket Guide. They'll point out helpful hints and let you know what to watch for.

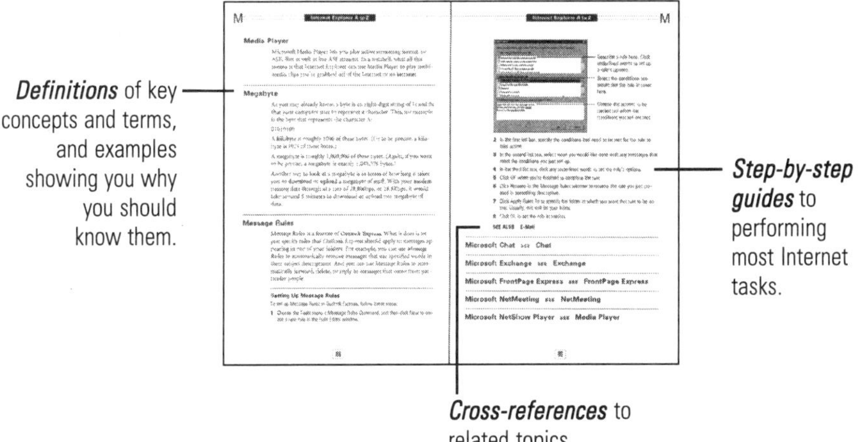

Definitions of key concepts and terms, and examples showing you why you should know them.
Step-by-step guides to performing most Internet tasks.
Cross-references to related topics.
Microsoft Chat see Chat
Microsoft Exchange see Exchange
Microsoft FrontPage Express see FrontPage Express
Microsoft NetMeeting see NetMeeting
Microsoft NetShow Player see Media Player

Introduction

This Pocket Guide provides quick, practical answers to just about any question you have about Internet Explorer. To acquaint yourself with this convenient and easy-to-use book, take two minutes now and read the Introduction. It explains how this unusual little book works.

What Is a Pocket Guide?

One of the problems with the larger books about computers is, quite frankly, their size. With a large book, you must typically sift through pages of information to find that one bit you need. And not only that, you've also got their physical size to contend with. It's rarely enjoyable and often not practical to lug around a thousand-page book if you're working both at home and at the office. Or if you're on the road with your laptop.

The *Microsoft Pocket Guide to Microsoft Internet Explorer 5* addresses both "size" problems of the larger computer books. Most obvious, of course, is the fact that this book is smaller. So it's easier to carry the book around wherever you go.

But this Pocket Guide also addresses the problem of wading through a large book to find the bit of information you need. And it does so in a variety of ways. For starters, this Pocket Guide organizes its information using an A to Z scheme—just like a dictionary or an encyclopedia does. This Pocket Guide supplies visual indexes in its Environment section, so you can find help even if you don't know how to describe what it is you're looking for. Finally, this Pocket Guide also uses a rich cross-referencing scheme that points you to related topics, tasks, or techniques.

For new users, the Pocket Guide provides the essential information necessary to start using Internet Explorer. And for experienced users, the Pocket Guide provides concise, easy-to-find descriptions of Internet Explorer tasks, terms, and techniques.

When You Have a Question

Let me explain how to find the information you need. If Internet Explorer is new to you, flip first to the Environment section, which is really a visual index. Find the picture that shows what you want to do or the task you have a question about. For example, if you want to know how to connect to the Internet, flip to pages 4 and 5, which talk about different ways to connect your personal computer to the Internet.

Next read the captions that describe the parts of the picture. Say, for example, that you want to use an Internet service provider. On page 4, there's a caption that describes what Internet service providers are.

You'll notice that some captions use **boldface** terms or are followed by additional boldface terms. These refer to entries in the second section, Internet Explorer A to Z, and provide more information related to the caption's contents.

Internet Explorer A to Z is a dictionary of more than 200 entries that define terms and describe tasks. (After you've worked with the Internet a bit or if you're already an experienced user, you'll often be able to turn directly to this section.) So if you have just read the caption in the Environment section that talks about Internet service providers, you'll see the term **Connection Wizard** in boldface, indicating a cross-reference. If you don't know what the Connection Wizard is, you can flip to the Connection Wizard entry in Internet Explorer A to Z.

When an entry in Internet Explorer A to Z appears as a term within another entry, I'll often **boldface** it the first time it appears in that entry. For example, as part of describing what the Connection Wizard is, I might tell you that after you run the Connection Wizard, you should be able to browse the **World Wide Web.** In this case, the words World Wide Web appear in bold letters—alerting you to the presence of another entry explaining the term World Wide Web. If you don't understand the term or want to do a bit of brushing up, you can flip to the entry for more information.

When You Have a Problem

The third section, Troubleshooting, describes problems that new and casual users of Internet Explorer often encounter. Following each problem description, I list one or more solutions you can employ to fix the problem.

When You Wonder About a Command

The Quick Reference at the end of the Pocket Guide describes the **Internet Explorer** and **Outlook Express** menu commands and toolbar buttons. If you want to know what a specific command or toolbar button does, turn to the Quick Reference. Don't forget about the Index either. You can look there to find all references in this book to any single topic.

Conventions Used Here

I have developed a few conventions to make using this book easier for you. Rather than use wordy phrases such as "Activate the File menu, and then choose the Print command" to describe how you choose a menu command, I'm just going to say, "Choose the File menu's Print command."

Also, I've rather freely tossed out uniform resource locators, or **URLs.** And to make them stand out on the page, I've *italicized* them. OK, now I know that you might not know what URLs are yet. But after you've experimented a bit—and learned how to use them—you'll be happy I provided them. They give you the precise directions for finding useful sites on the Internet.

Here's another convention: To make dialog box button and box labels stand out, I've capitalized the initial letter of each word in the label. I think this makes it easier to understand an instruction such as "Check the Print To File box." With this scheme, it's easier to see, for example, that "Print To File" is a label.

Finally, I want to let you know about a couple of conventions I used when creating the figures for this book so that you won't get confused if the figures you see here look a little different than the figures you see on your screen. First, you might notice that all of the web pages you see in this book include the Internet Explorer application window, instead of taking up the whole screen. This is because I find the menu bar and the Microsoft Windows Taskbar handy when I'm working in Internet Explorer, so I like to keep them displayed. If you agree with me, you can click the Fullscreen toolbar button to switch out of full screen mode. The other thing I want to say about the figures in this book is that they might look a little different than what you have on your screen depending on which version of Internet Explorer you installed. This book applies to all of the versions but when I was writing this book, I used the full installation, which is why you might see some buttons or features here that you didn't install.

Environment

Need to get oriented quickly? Then the Environment is the place to start. It defines the key terms you'll need to know and the core ideas you should understand as you begin using Internet Explorer 5.

What Is the Internet?

The Internet is a collection of networks that speak the same language, or to put it another way, use the same protocol.

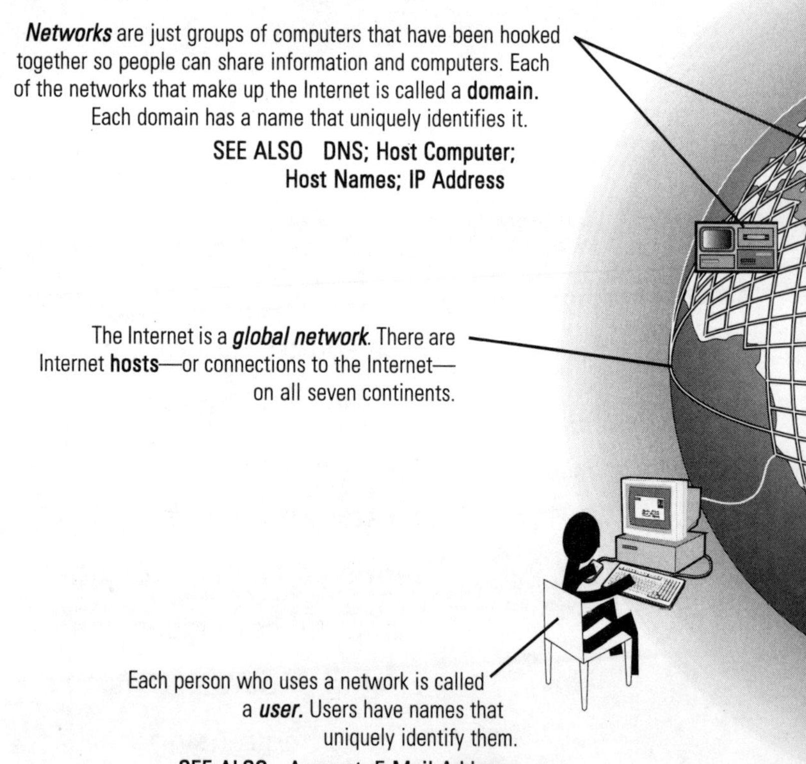

Networks are just groups of computers that have been hooked together so people can share information and computers. Each of the networks that make up the Internet is called a **domain.** Each domain has a name that uniquely identifies it.

SEE ALSO **DNS; Host Computer; Host Names; IP Address**

The Internet is a ***global network***. There are Internet **hosts**—or connections to the Internet—on all seven continents.

Each person who uses a network is called a ***user.*** Users have names that uniquely identify them.

SEE ALSO **Account; E-Mail Address; Username**

The Internet is a global network of networks. This "network of networks" lets people who are connected share information and, in special situations, share computing **resources** too. Electronic mail is the most popular Internet service. But it isn't the only one. Using the Internet, people can share, or transfer, anything that can be stored in a **file**: text, a picture, or a program. Using a feature called **Telnet,** people can **log on** (connect) to and use other computer systems.

Host-to-host connections use a variety of technologies: regular old telephone lines, high-speed, dedicated data-transmission lines, satellites, microwave links, and even fiber-optic cables.

SEE ALSO T1 Transmission Line; T3 Transmission Line

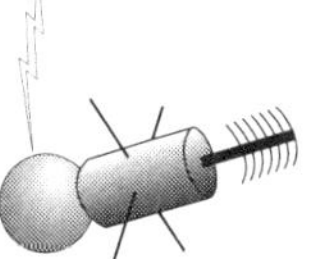

Connecting to the Internet

To use any resource or service on the Internet, you first need to connect to it.

Users with ***accounts*** on existing Internet **hosts** are already connected. If you work for a university or a large business, you may be connected already.

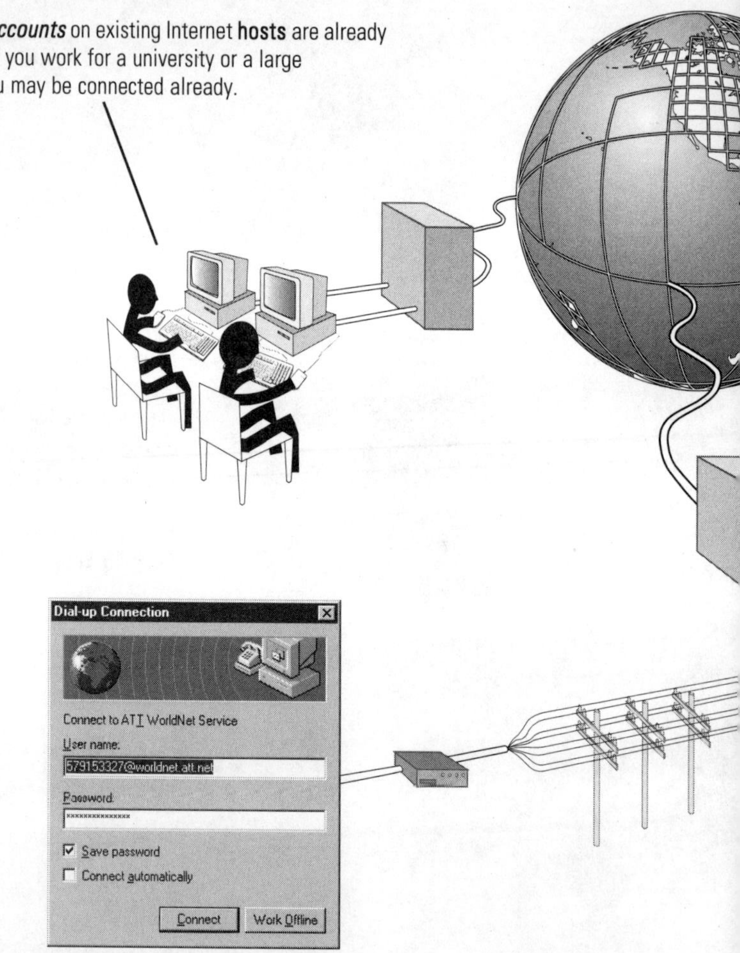

Internet service providers offer pay-for-use accounts on computers that are connected directly to the Internet. With a modem and a personal computer, you can often connect to a local service provider.

SEE ALSO Connection Wizard; Dial-Up Networking; Shell Account

People get connected in a variety of ways. The cheapest and easiest way to get connected is to use your personal computer and **modem** to connect by way of an **Internet service provider.** The most expensive, most complicated, and most powerful way to get connected, or "wired," is to have your network become one of the Internet's permanent networks.

SEE ALSO Connection Wizard

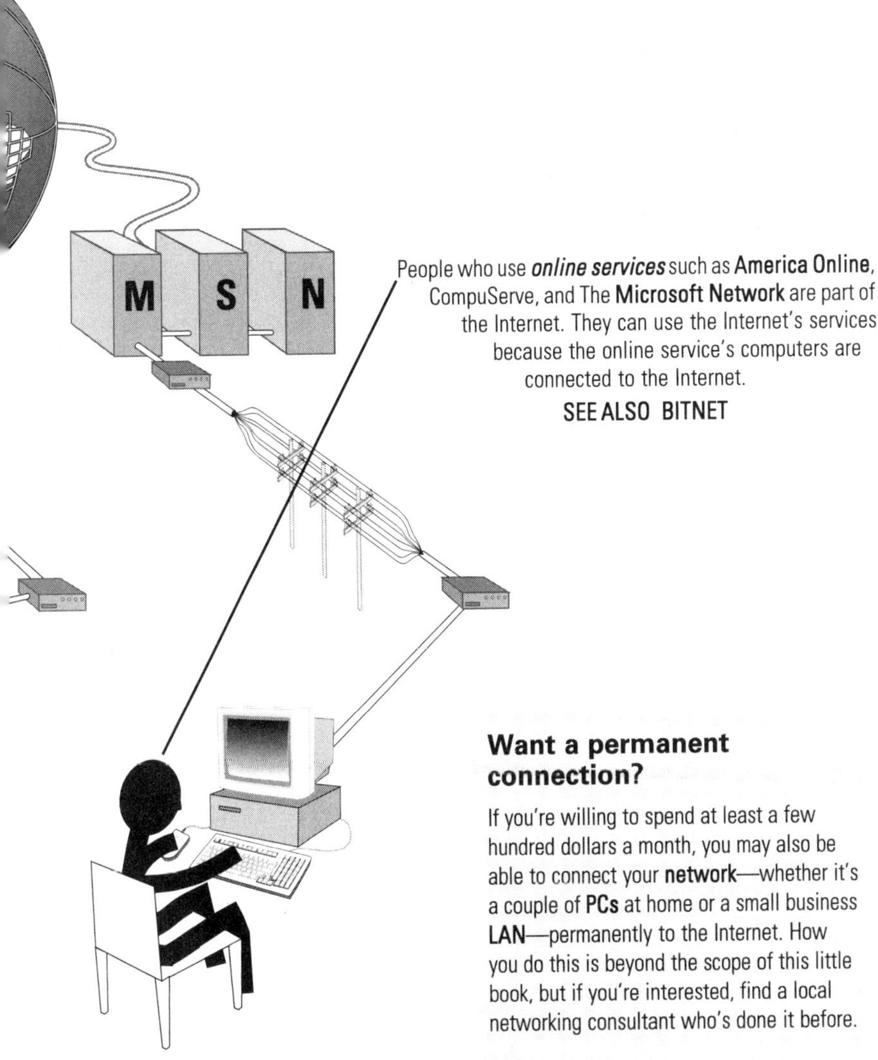

People who use ***online services*** such as **America Online**, CompuServe, and The **Microsoft Network** are part of the Internet. They can use the Internet's services, because the online service's computers are connected to the Internet.

SEE ALSO BITNET

Want a permanent connection?

If you're willing to spend at least a few hundred dollars a month, you may also be able to connect your **network**—whether it's a couple of **PCs** at home or a small business **LAN**—permanently to the Internet. How you do this is beyond the scope of this little book, but if you're interested, find a local networking consultant who's done it before.

Sending Electronic Mail

The Internet's most popular service is electronic mail, or e-mail.

E-mail programs such as **Outlook Express** let you create and send mail messages. They also let you read and organize mail messages others send you.

Addresses give the names of both the **user** and host.

SEE ALSO Domain Names; E-Mail Address

Interest lists are electronic **mailing lists** of people who have a special interest in a specific topic. By joining an interest list—putting your name on the mailing list—you can see tons of messages related to a topic.

SEE ALSO FAQ; Lurk; Netiquette

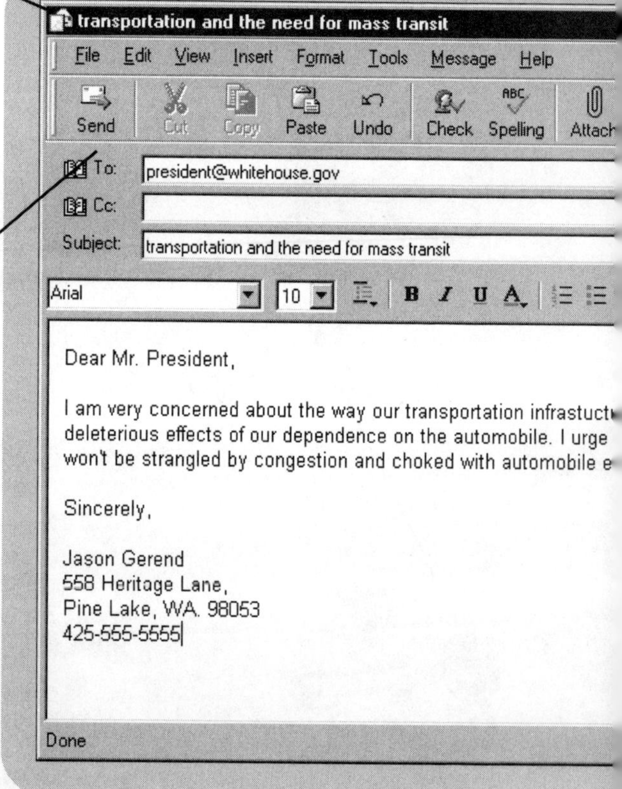

To send someone electronic mail, you create a mail message. The message includes the name and **e-mail address** of the person to whom the message should be delivered, the text of the message, and your name and e-mail address. Once you send your message, it is passed from **host** to host until the message reaches its destination.

Mail **gateways** connect the Internet to other networks such as **America Online** and CompuServe, so you can send mail messages to users of these services, too.

SEE ALSO E-Mail; Outlook Express

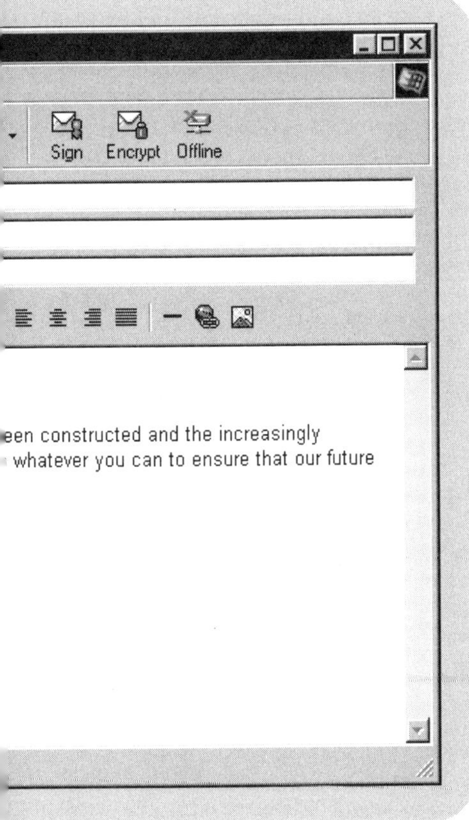

How secure are e-mail messages?

It's not easy to intercept e-mail messages, and most people wouldn't intercept others' mail intentionally, but you should know it is possible to eavesdrop on e-mail messages. For this reason, some people **encrypt** messages.

Newsgroups

Newsgroups resemble interest lists. In newsgroups, mail messages are collected and organized by topic. The difference is that newsgroup mail messages, called **articles,** aren't distributed but are stored on central computers, called news **servers.** You decide which newsgroup articles you want to read—they aren't sent to you.

World Wide Web

The World Wide Web is a collection of multimedia documents that are connected by hyperlinks.

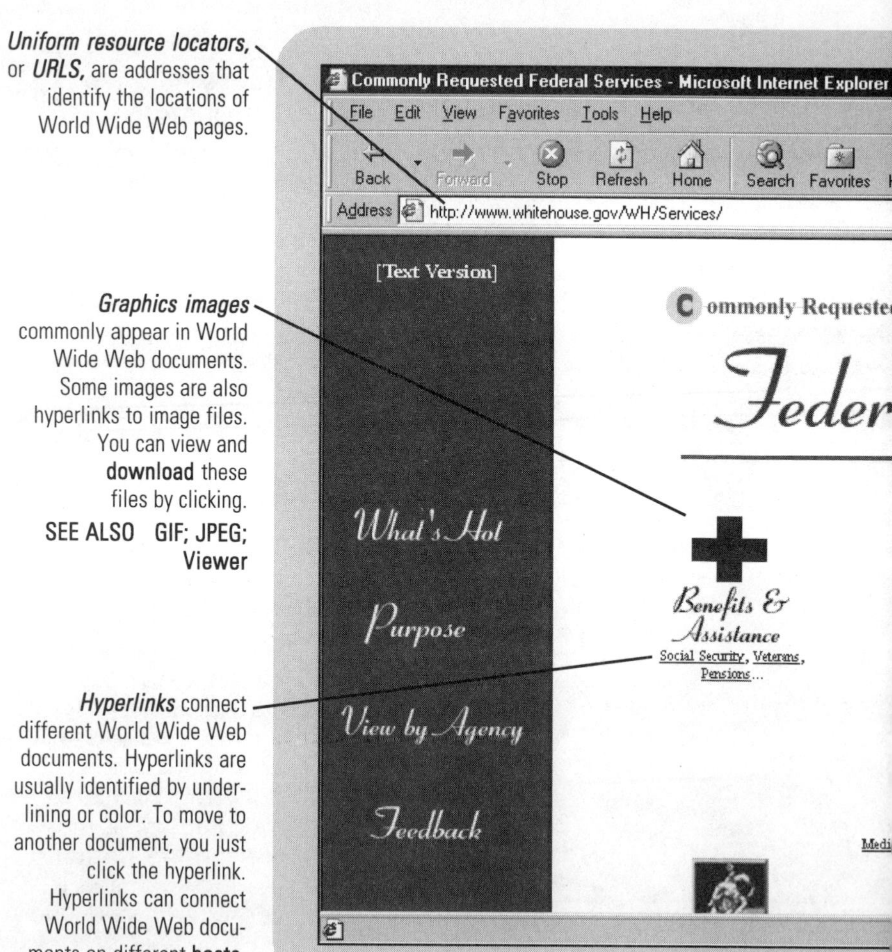

Uniform resource locators, or ***URLS,*** are addresses that identify the locations of World Wide Web pages.

Graphics images commonly appear in World Wide Web documents. Some images are also hyperlinks to image files. You can view and **download** these files by clicking.

SEE ALSO GIF; JPEG; **Viewer**

Hyperlinks connect different World Wide Web documents. Hyperlinks are usually identified by underlining or color. To move to another document, you just click the hyperlink. Hyperlinks can connect World Wide Web documents on different **hosts.**

To view **World Wide Web** documents, you need a web **browser,** such as Microsoft **Internet Explorer,** and a **Dial-Up Networking** connection or an account on an **online service** that provides World Wide Web browsing. You browse web pages by clicking hyperlinks and entering URLs. You can also tell Internet Explorer to automatically download **offline pages** for viewing while disconnected from the Internet.

Toolbars in Internet Explorer provide buttons you can click to navigate the World Wide Web and make use of other Internet features. Which toolbar buttons you have depends on how you installed Internet Explorer.

SEE ALSO **Installing or Upgrading Internet Explorer**

World Wide Web documents can include text, pictures, and just about anything else that can be stored in a computer **file.**

File Transfers

File transfers represent another way to share information on the Internet.

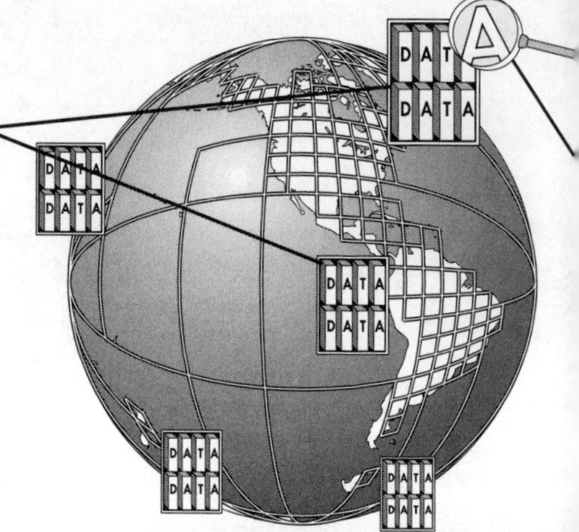

Data archives exist all over the world. Using the Internet, you should be able to access publicly accessible data archives.

SEE ALSO Anonymous FTP; Netiquette

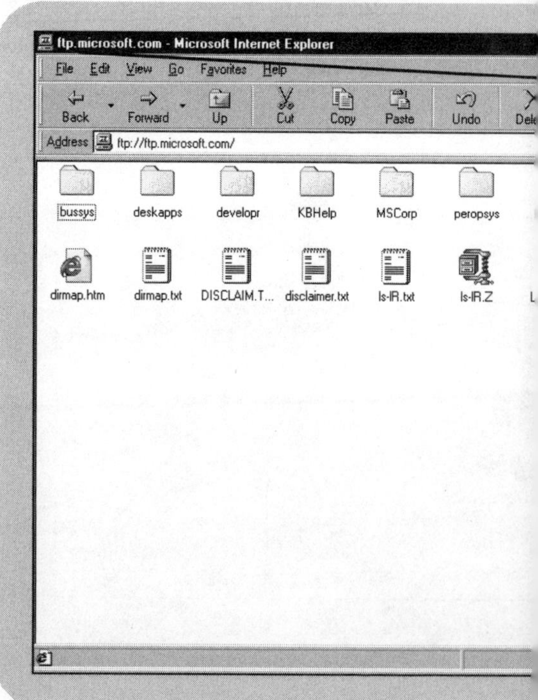

Compression utilities shrink files so they take less time to transmit over the Internet. When you receive a file that has been compressed, you need to decompress ("unshrink") it.

SEE ALSO Bandwidth; Bits; PKZIP; ZIP

File transfers let you copy files between Internet hosts. To transfer files between Internet hosts, you use the file transfer protocol, or **FTP.** You can copy almost anything that can be stored in a **file**: programs (for a variety of computers and operating systems), images, and, of course, plain text files.

File location tools such as **Archie** and **search engines** make it easier to find files you want—even if it means you need to search **hosts** all over the world.

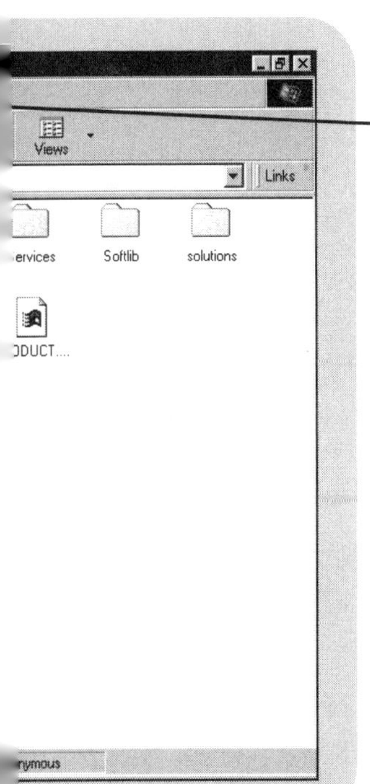

File retrieval usually requires you to start a **client,** such as **Internet Explorer,** and then to issue a command indicating that you want to get a file. To retrieve a file with FTP using Internet Explorer, you just double-click the file's name in a list.

SEE ALSO **Downloading Files**

Telnetting

Internet Explorer also allows you to remotely connect, or log on, to other Internet hosts.

You use ***telnet*** to connect to another Internet **host.** Once you connect to the other host, you log on by providing a **username** and a **password**.

Menu systems usually appear once you successfully log on to the other Internet host. Menu systems guide you through the services you can use.

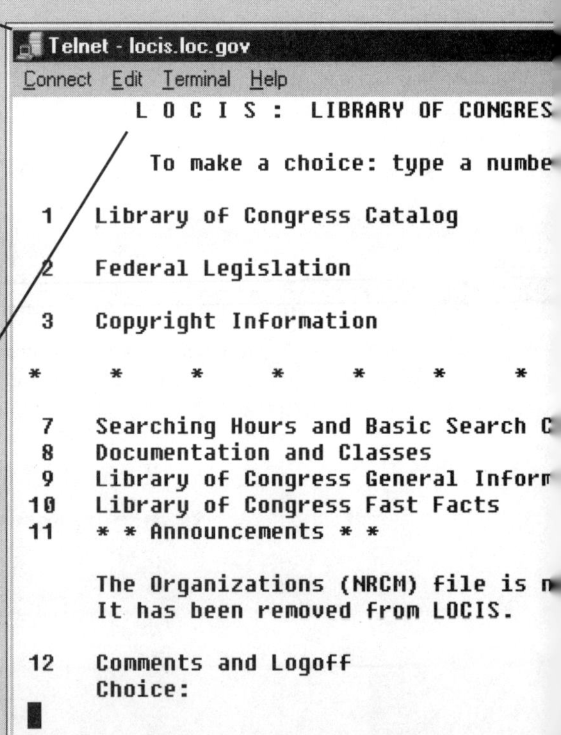

Once you've logged on, you can use the other computer system—or at least the parts of it you're allowed to use. One important factor to keep in mind is that computers and networks operate in different environments. So things may look a bit different once you connect. For example, if you're used to working in Microsoft Windows and you **telnet** to a **UNIX** network, the screens and the commands will look different. If you've telnetted to a different country, you may even see a different language.

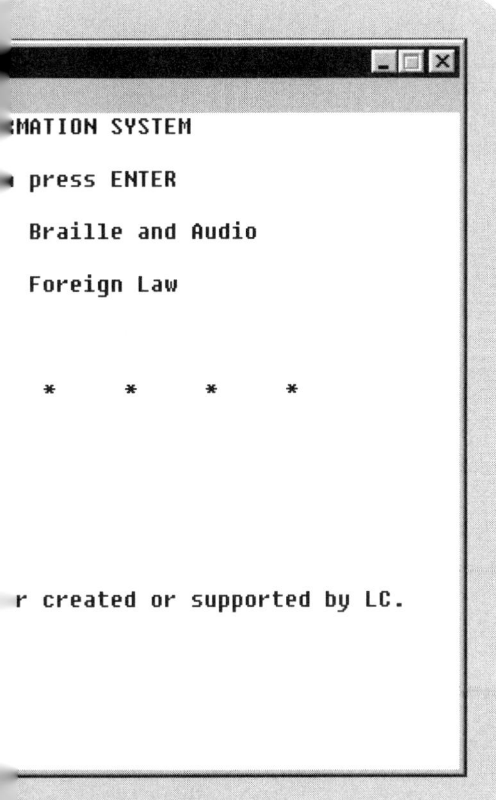

Making a ***telnet connection*** typically requires you to click a **hyperlink** that points to a telnet site or to supply the **URL** for a telnet site.

Three telnet tips

When you telnet to another host, you should pay particular attention to three things: how you should disconnect once you're done, how to get help within the system, and the name and **e-mail address** of the person you should contact if a problem arises.

Internet Explorer

A to Z

When you have a question, you want a quick, easy answer. Internet Explorer A to Z, which starts on the next page, should provide just these sorts of answers. It lists in alphabetic order the tools, terms, and techniques you'll need to know.

Access Provider SEE Internet Service Provider

Account

To use an **Internet service provider,** you typically sign up for an account. This account, in effect, is how you identify yourself to the Internet service provider's **host computer.** As part of setting up your account, the system administrator gives you a **username** that you use to identify yourself to the system and a **password** so that you can get into the system.

Acrobat Reader

The Acrobat Reader **viewer** is used to open Portable Document Format (PDF) files. PDF files are like web pages, except they can have more complex layouts and graphics. If you come across a PDF file and you do not already have Acrobat Reader installed, look for a **hyperlink** that leads you to a location where you can download the free viewer. If you can't find the hyperlink, head over to Adobe Systems Incorporated at *www.adobe.com.*

Active Channel

An active channel is a channel web site that you've specified as one you want to regularly view. By making the channel active, the channel web site will regularly deliver content to your computer. You can view a channel in the Microsoft Internet Explorer browser window, as a full screen window, on an **Active Desktop,** or as a screen saver.

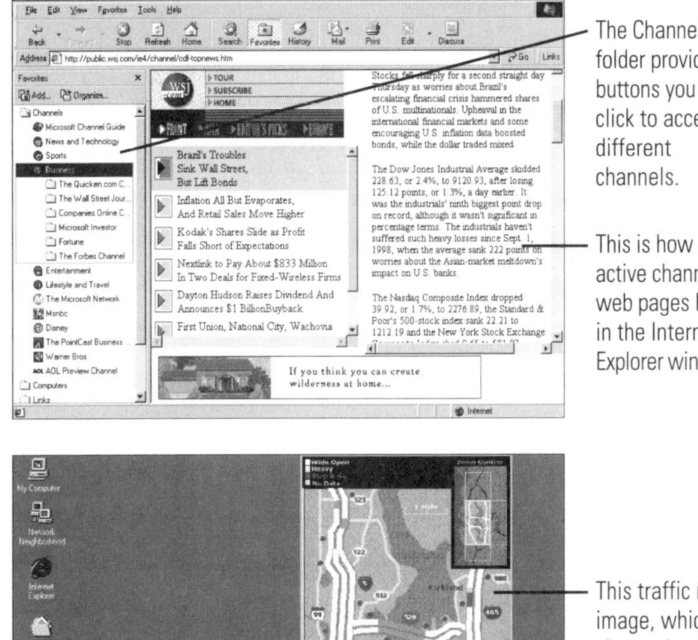

The Channels folder provides buttons you can click to access different channels.

This is how an active channel's web pages look in the Internet Explorer window.

This traffic map image, which sits on the Microsoft Windows desktop, is also an active channel.

SEE ALSO Web Browsing

Active Desktop

An Active Desktop is a Windows **desktop** that you've essentially turned into one, big **web page.** Let me explain this a bit more. The screen that you see after you start (and possibly log on to) Windows is the Windows desktop. This desktop, as you probably know, shows the Start button, the Taskbar, and clickable shortcut icons you can use to start programs or view Windows folders.

continues

Active Desktop *(continued)*

An Active Desktop is a sort-of supercharged desktop to which you've added a web page background or some portion of a web page—perhaps from a **channel.** With an Active Desktop, you can display web pages, or at least pieces of them, right on your desktop. You can also use a web page as your desktop background (also known as wallpaper).

Adding Items to Your Desktop with an Add To Active Desktop Button

To add a web page to your Active Desktop, display the web page that you want to add. Then click the web page's Add To Active Desktop button. (You may need to hunt about a bit for this button.) Internet Explorer adds the web page to your Active Desktop as an Active **Desktop item.**

Adding Items to Your Desktop Without the Add To Active Desktop Button

To add an item to your Active Desktop for a web page that doesn't show an Add To Active Desktop button, follow these steps:

1. Right-click the Active Desktop.
2. Choose the Properties command. Windows displays the Display Properties dialog box.
3. Click the Web tab.

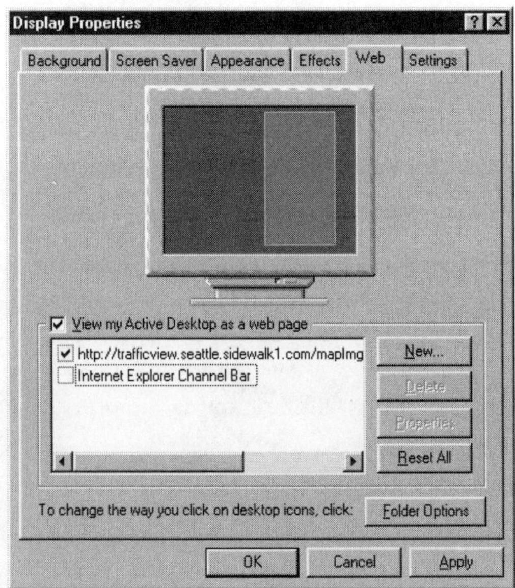

4 Click New.

5 When Windows asks you if you'd like to go to the Active Desktop gallery to preview and install desktop items, click No to set up the specific web page you want.

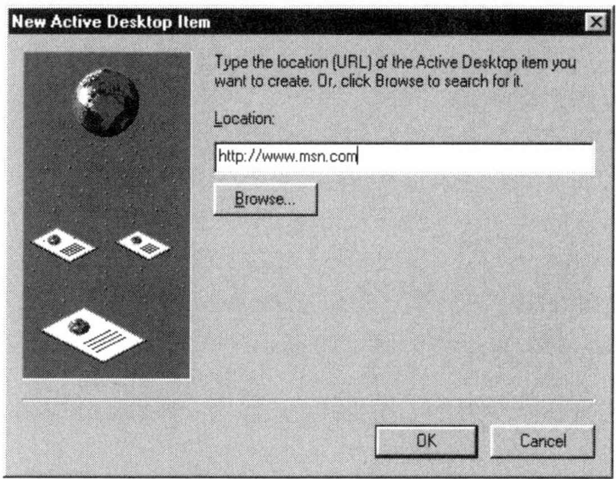

6 When Windows prompts you, enter the **URL** of the web page you want to use as a desktop item on your Active Desktop. Click OK when you are asked to confirm the addition of the new desktop item.

Updating Desktop Items

To update the desktop items shown on your Active Desktop, right-click the desktop to display the Active Desktop shortcut menu. Choose the Active Desktop command to display the Active Desktop submenu. Then choose the Update Now command.

About the Active Desktop submenu's other commands

The Active Desktop submenu also provides two other commands. The View As Web Page command, which works like a toggle switch, lets you alternately view your Active Desktop as a Windows desktop or as a web page in a browser window. (Experiment with this command to see how it works.) The Customize My Desktop command displays the Display Properties dialog box.

continues

Active Desktop *(continued)*

Removing Desktop Items

To remove a desktop item from your Active Desktop, follow these steps:

1 Right-click the Active Desktop.

2 Choose the Properties command. Windows displays the Display Properties dialog box.

3 Click the Web tab.

4 Click the desktop item you want to remove.

5 Click Delete.

Using an HTML Document for Desktop Wallpaper

To use an HTML document you've stored locally on your computer as wallpaper, or background, follow these steps:

1 Right-click the Active Desktop.

2 Choose the Properties command. Windows displays the Display Properties dialog box.

3 Click the Background tab.

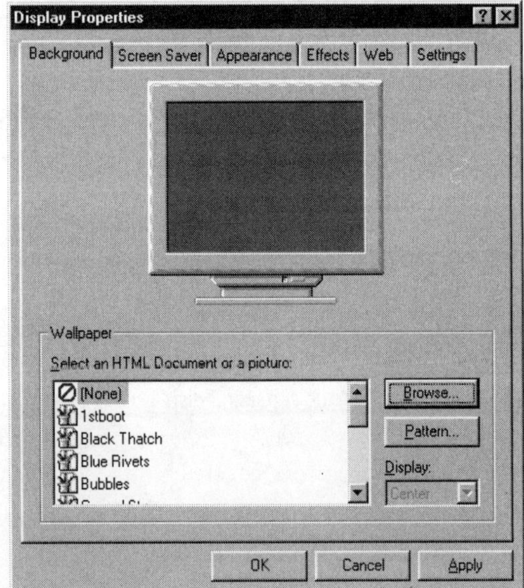

4 Click Browse. Windows displays the Open dialog box.

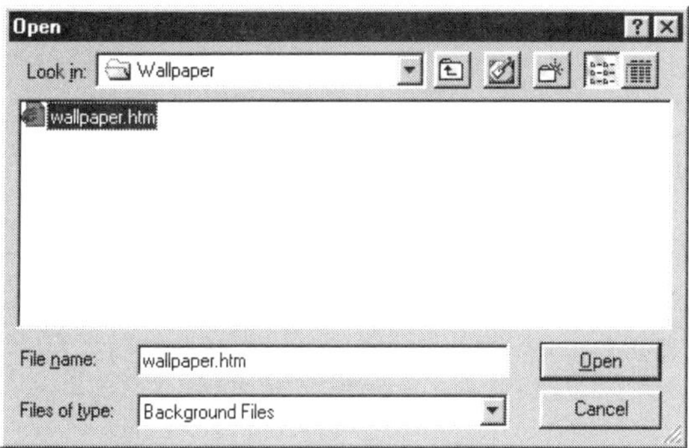

5 Use the Open dialog box's buttons and boxes to locate the HTML document.

6 Double-click the HTML document. Windows adds the HTML document to the list box that shows available wallpaper selections for your Active Desktop.

7 Select the HTML document from the Wallpaper list box.

8 Click OK.

Removing or Replacing HTML Wallpaper

You can easily remove or replace an HTML document you've used for wallpaper. To remove wallpaper from the desktop background, click the Background tab in the Display Properties dialog box (as described in the preceding instructions), select the None entry from the Wallpaper list box, and click OK. (The None entry appears at the top of the list.)

To replace the existing HTML wallpaper with some other wallpaper, click the Background tab in the Display Properties dialog box and then select another wallpaper from the Wallpaper list box. After you've made your selection, click OK.

Active Server Pages

Sometimes the address for the **web page** you're viewing doesn't end with the .htm or .html extension. Instead it ends with an .asp extension. The .asp extension means that the page has been created dynamically by an active server computer program; hence the Active Server Page (.asp) extension. It's just another kind of web page.

SEE ALSO **Web Page**

ActiveX

ActiveX is the name Microsoft has given to a technology that lets people share information and programs. Using ActiveX, for example, you can view a Microsoft Word word-processor document with Internet Explorer. You can move information you create from one program (such as Microsoft Excel) to another program (such as Microsoft PowerPoint). And you can run miniature ActiveX programs inside a web browser such as Internet Explorer. Well, I should say, you can if the browser supports ActiveX technology.

Address Bar

You use the Address bar to type the **URL** for the web site you want to open. In Internet Explorer and Windows Explorer, the Address bar is smart; oftentimes it will fill in the gaps for you using the AutoComplete feature. You can also use a **search engine** directly from the Address bar by typing *find* and then your search word or phrase. You can turn on the Address bar, if it's not already on, by right-clicking it on the Standard **toolbar** and then choosing the Address Bar command.

Rearranging the Address bar and other toolbars

You can arrange the Address bar, the Standard toolbar, the Links bar, and the Menu bar in any order you want. Just click on the vertical line at the very left of the bar you'd like to move, and then drag it to the location where you'd like to place the bar.

Address Book

You use the Address Book to store the names and e-mail addresses of the people to whom you want to send **e-mail.** You can also store people's addresses, telephone numbers, and other information.

Opening the Address Book

To open the Address Book, you typically first start Microsoft Outlook Express and then click the Address Book toolbar button. You can also open the Address Book from within Outlook Express by choosing the Tools menu's Address Book command. From within Internet Explorer, you open the Address Book by choosing the Go menu's Address Book command.

Storing an E-Mail Address

You can store an e-mail address in your Address Book in several ways. If you want to add the name of a person who has already sent you a message, display the message and right-click the sender's name. When Outlook Express displays the shortcut menu, choose the Add To Address Book command.

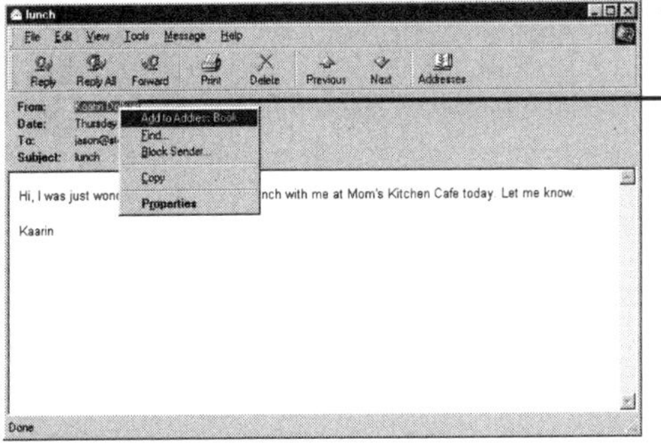

Right-click the sender's name in the message window to display a shortcut menu with a command for adding the sender's name to your Address Book.

If you haven't already received a message (or can't find a message) from the person you want to add to your Address Book, open the Address Book and then follow the steps on the next page.

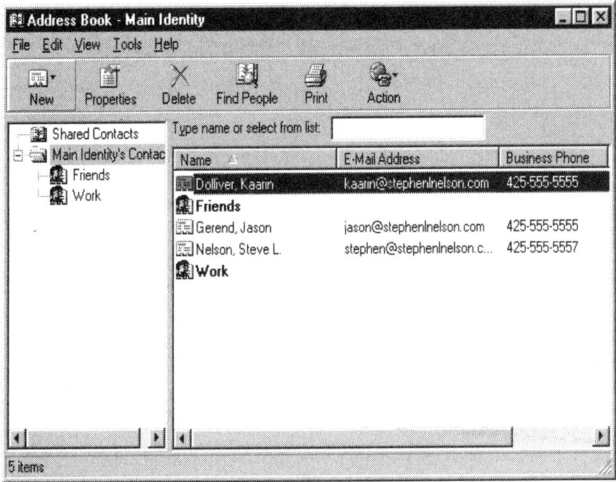

continues

Address Book *(continued)*

1 Click the New toolbar button. Choose the New Contact command from the menu that opens up. Outlook Express then displays the Properties dialog box.

2 Enter the person's name in the First, MIddle, Last, Display, and Nickname boxes. (The name you enter in the Display box shows up in your e-mail messages to that person.)

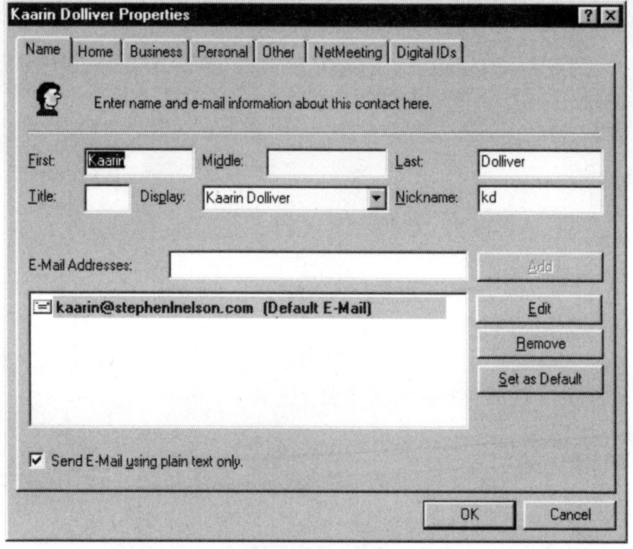

3 Enter the full e-mail address for the person in the E-Mail Addresses box, and then click Add.

4 Optionally, if this person uses an e-mail client that works with plain text only, select the Send E-Mail Using Plain Text Only check box.

5 Optionally, click the Home, Business, Personal, Other, NetMeeting, or Digital IDs tabs and use their buttons and boxes to describe the person in more detail.

6 When you finish describing the person, click OK.

Printing E-Mail Information

You can print the e-mail name and address information that you collect. To do this, in the Address Book window select the name of the person whose information you want to print. Then click Print.

Using an E-Mail Address in a Message

You can use e-mail address information from the Address Book in several ways. The simplest method is to enter the person's Display name in the To box in the new message form. (This is the name you entered in the Display box in step 3 in the preceding instructions.) When you do this, Outlook Express retrieves the e-mail address from the Address Book and then uses the e-mail address to send the message.

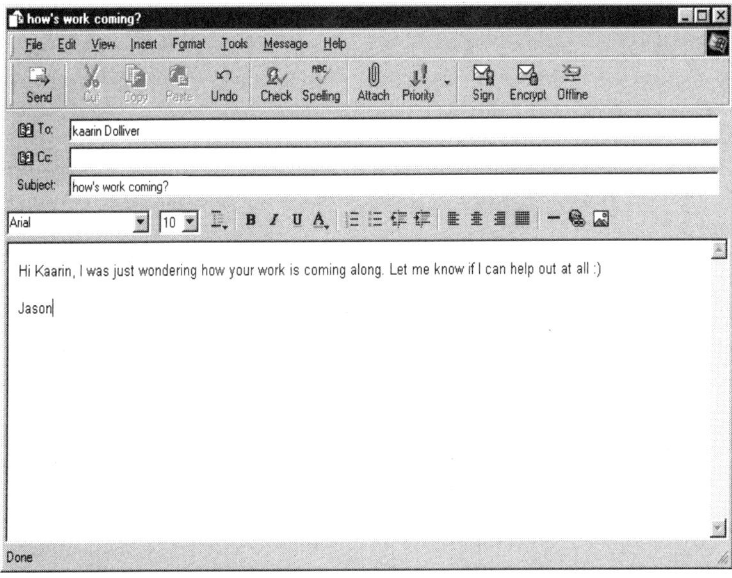

If you're not sure of the Display name you used, open the Address Book, select the name of the person to whom you want to send an e-mail message, click the Action toolbar button, and then choose the Send Mail command from the menu that opens up. Outlook Express opens a new message form and fills in the To box with the name of the person you selected. To complete your message, type the message subject, write the message, and click the Send toolbar button.

Updating or Deleting an E-Mail Address

To update e-mail address information you've stored in the Address Book, open the Address Book, select the e-mail address you want to change, and then click the Properties toolbar button. If you want to delete an e-mail address, click the e-mail address and then click the Delete toolbar button.

continues

Address Book *(continued)*

Importing E-Mail Addresses You've Stored in Another Client's Address Book

If prior to using Outlook Express you used another e-mail client, you may already have an address book of e-mail names and addresses. Fortunately, you may be able to extract this information from the other client's address book. To do this, follow these steps:

1. Start Outlook Express.
2. Choose the File menu's Import command, and then choose the Import submenu's Other Address Book command. Outlook Express displays the Address Book Import Tool dialog box.

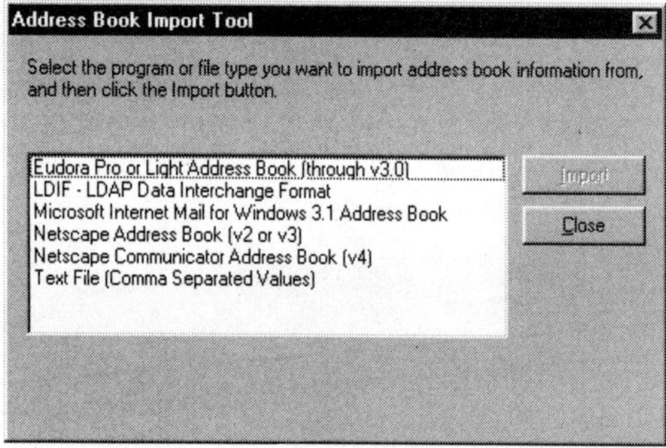

3. Select the list box entry that corresponds to the type of e-mail client and address book you previously used.
4. Click Import. Then follow the on-screen instructions. (The instructions vary depending on what you want to import.)

SEE ALSO Groups

ADSL SEE Asymmetric Digital Subscriber Line

AltaVista

AltaVista is an Internet **search engine,** or search service. It works like a giant index of the Internet. To use AltaVista, you specify a word or phrase you want to look up. (You do this using a search form, which is just a web page that provides boxes and buttons.) AltaVista then looks up the word or phrase in its index and displays a list of **hyperlinks** that point to web pages that use the term. To move to a page, you click its hyperlink. (For step-by-step instructions about how to use AltaVista and other search engines, refer to the search engine A to Z entry.)

Like other search engines, AltaVista makes it possible for you to find information on the **World Wide Web.** For this reason, you'll definitely want to learn how to use AltaVista or one of the other search engines.

SEE ALSO **Yahoo!**

America Online

America Online is one of many online services that gives you access to a lot of different resources, including the Internet. However, I'm not going to describe how you access the Internet specifically with America Online (or any other **Internet service provider**) in this book.

I will say that if you want to **e-mail** someone who subscribes to America Online, you just need to tag the America Online **domain name,** aol.com, onto the end of his or her **username.** So a person with an America Online account will have the following **e-mail address:** *username@aol.com* with the username being replaced with the unique name they chose.

SEE ALSO **Netiquette**

Anchor

The **hyperlinks** in **World Wide Web** documents—the same ones you click to move from web page to web page—are sometimes called anchors. I don't really know why. But then I don't make the rules.

Anonymous FTP

Anonymous FTP just means that someone without an **account** on an Internet **host** can still **FTP.** In other words, if an Internet host allows anonymous FTPs, you can connect to the host (no matter who you are) and start FTPing.

Using Internet Explorer for Anonymous FTP

To use anonymous FTP, simply enter the **URL** of the FTP site in the Address box of Internet Explorer. When you do, Internet Explorer displays the FTP site's folders, or directories. The FTP site looks just like any other folder on your hard drive; however, you won't be able to change any of the site's files or directories.

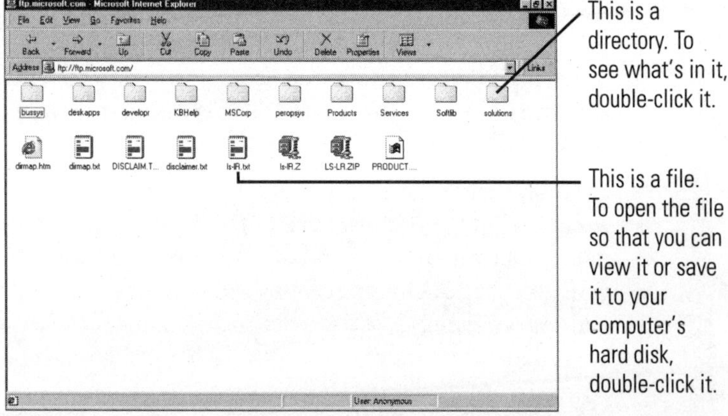

List of Useful Anonymous FTP Sites

There are a bunch of anonymous FTP sites. I can't list them all, but here's a starter list of URLs that you can use to track down and explore some of the more popular and useful FTP sites for Windows users:

URL	What the site offers
ftp://ftp.microsoft.com	Selected Microsoft Corporation programs including several for Windows
ftp://ftp.ncsa.uiuc.edu	National Center for Supercomputing Applications stuff from the University of Illinois at Urbana-Champaign—such as the NCSA Mosaic web browser
ftp://rtfm.mit.edu	**FAQs** maintained by the Massachusetts Institute of Technology on just about everything

SEE ALSO **FTP**

Apple Macintosh

The world of microcomputers is essentially divided into two camps, the Apple Macintosh camp and the PC camp. PC stands for personal computer, and although Macintoshes are also personal computers, the term *PC* always refers to IBM computers and IBM compatibles.

This book focuses on connecting PCs that are running Windows 95, Windows 98, and Windows NT 4 or later to the Internet. You won't find anything here specifically about Apple Macintosh computers, or "Macs" as they are called by their loyal users. But much of what I say here also applies to Mac users.

Archie

Archie is a tool people use for finding **files** at **FTP** sites. In essence, what you do is tell Archie that you're interested in files with a specific name or files that have a specified string in their names (a string is just a block of text). Archie goes out and looks through a list of files at an Archie **server.** Then it builds a list of files (and their locations) that match your description and sends you the list. If you see something you want to retrieve, you use **anonymous FTP** to retrieve the file. Archie was popular before the rise of the **World Wide Web,** but with files so easy to find nowadays on the Web, not many people use Archie anymore. Nevertheless, Archie is still a useful and powerful tool, so I'll tell you a little bit about how to use Archie, just in case you ever need it.

continues

Archie *(continued)*

Using Archie with E-Mail

Windows users have several ways to use Archie. One method is to send an **e-mail** message to one of the Archie servers. To do this, you need to find out the **domain name** of an Archie server. For example, maybe you discover there's an Archie server named *archie.rutgers.edu.* (There actually is an Archie server with this domain name.) Once you have this information, send an e-mail message to Archie at the Archie server. For example, to send an e-mail to archie.rutgers.edu, you send the e-mail to *archie@archie.rutgers.edu.* Oh, one other thing. Your e-mail message needs to use the message text

```
find filename
```

The **filename** should be either the filename or a portion of the filename. For example, if you want to find files that use the word "mouse," your message text is

```
find mouse
```

A little while later—it could easily be an hour—you'll get back an e-mail message that lists **URLs** for files that use the word or string you specified. You then use FTP to retrieve the file you want.

Using Archie with Telnet

If you installed the Windows **telnet** client on your computer, the simplest method for finding files with an Archie server is to telnet to the Archie server (**netiquette** says you should almost always use one that's close to your host), sign on using Archie as the **username** but without a **password,** and then use its commands. After you've telnetted to the Archie server and you see the Archie command prompt, for example, enter the *find* command:

```
find filename
```

Finding an Archie Server

You need to know an Archie server's domain name before you can send it e-mail or try to telnet to it, of course. On the next page you'll find a list of Archie servers that were active as I was writing this book.

Server	Location
archie.au	Australia
archie.univie.ac.at	Austria
archie.belnet.be	Belgium
archie.bunyip.com	Canada
archie.cs.mcgill.ca	Canada
archie.funet.fi	Finland
archie.cru.fr	France
archie.th-darmstadt.de	Germany
archie.ac.il	Israel
archie.unipi.it	Italy
archie.wide.ad.jp	Japan
archie.hana.nm.kr	Korea
archie.kornet.nm.kr	Korea
archie.sogang.ac.kr	Korea
archie.nz	New Zealand
archie.uninett.no	Norway
archie.icm.edu.pl	Poland
archie.rediris.es	Spain
archie.luth.se	Sweden
archie.switch.ch	Switzerland
archie.ncu.edu.tw	Taiwan
archie.doc.ic.ac.uk	United Kingdom
archie.hensa.ac.uk	United Kingdom
archie.sura.net	USA (Maryland)
archie.unl.edu	USA (Nebraska)
archie.internic.net	USA (New Jersey)
archie.rutgers.edu	USA (New Jersey)
archie.ans.net	USA (New York)

Getting an up-to-date list of Archie servers

You can get a list of active Archie servers like the one shown above by sending the one-word message "servers" to an Archie server.

continues

Archie *(continued)*

Using Archie with Internet Explorer

Not surprisingly, several web servers also maintain Archie server catalogs. These web servers provide web page forms that let you search their catalogs. To use this method for locating a file with Archie, use a **search engine** such as AltaVista to build a current list of Archie catalog web sites. (To do this, search on the term "Archie.") Then click the appropriate hyperlink to get the closest Archie web server, and follow its on-screen instructions.

ARPA

ARPA is an acronym for Advanced Research Projects Agency. ARPA is the central research and development agency for the U.S. Department of Defense. You're wondering, of course, what any of this has to do with the Internet. Well, quite a lot actually. Over the past 20 years, ARPA funded many computer-related projects that shaped the computer industry and the Internet. BSD (Berkeley Software Distribution) **UNIX** is one example, and the **TCP/IP** protocol is another. Most significant, however, is the fact that ARPA funded the ARPANET **network** that served as the starting point of the Internet.

Article

People often call the messages that get posted to a **newsgroup** "articles." This name makes sense if you think of a newsgroup as an electronic newspaper or magazine. If newspapers and magazines contain articles, so too must newsgroups.

If people respond to an article by posting other articles, the first article and its responses are called a **thread.**

Asymmetric Digital Subscriber Line

Asymmetric Digital Subscriber Line, or ADSL, is a new type of super-fast telephone connection that lets you connect to the Internet at the same time you talk on the phone or use a fax machine. ADSL works by sending highly compressed digital data across a standard, analog telephone line, just like **ISDN.** ADSL is much better at compressing data than ISDN, which makes it much faster. (ADSL can download up to 8Mbps vs. ISDN's 128Kbps.)

Unlike ISDN, ADSL is asymmetric, which means that you download files from the Internet or your corporate network much faster (up to 8Mbps) than you can upload them (up to 1Mbps). In order to use ADSL, both your phone company and your **Internet service provider** must support it.

SEE ALSO ISDN

Authentication

Authentication refers to the process by which an Internet service provider's **host computer** makes sure that you and your computer are who you say you are. You can't just **log on** to an **Internet service provider's** host computer. You have to provide your name or a **username.** And you need to provide a **password.**

AVI

AVI stands for Audio Video Interleaved and is Microsoft's standard file format for video clips. **Internet Explorer** can display AVI files either inside the web **browser** or in a separate window using the Windows Media Player.

Backbone

The term *backbone* refers to the extremely fast, high-bandwidth connections over which a majority of Internet traffic moves. In the United States of America, SprintNet (a commercial firm) maintains the backbone, although not all that long ago NSFnet (a government agency) maintained the backbone. Other countries typically have their own backbones.

Bandwidth

When people talk about the Internet, they use the term *bandwidth* to describe how much data can be transmitted in a given time, say a second. In these cases, people usually calibrate the bandwidth in **bits per second** (bps), kilobits per second (Kbps), or megabits per second (Mbps).

SEE ALSO Asymmetric Digital Subscriber Line; Bit; Cable Modem; ISDN; T1 Transmission Line; T3 Transmission Line

Baud

Baud (rhymes with "Maude") is the measure of data-transmission speed. When it comes to **modem** speeds, people often talk about the "baud rate," although modem speed is not measured in bauds. Actually, modem speed is measured by the number of data bits that can be transmitted in a second. That is, modem speed is measured in **bits per second** (bps), kilobits per second (Kbps), or megabits per second (Mbps).

SEE ALSO **Asymmetric Digital Subscriber Line; Cable Modem; ISDN; Modem**

BBS

BBS is an acronym for bulletin board system. In essence, BBSs work like those cork bulletin boards you see at the local grocery store. You know the ones I mean, right? The same ones where ancient Winnebagos are offered for sale, where 12-year-old kids offer babysitting services, and rewards are offered for lost dogs.

The only difference between cork bulletin boards and BBSs is that you post and read BBS messages electronically by using your computer and a **modem.** All you need is a communications program like Windows's **HyperTerminal** application to connect to a BBS. If you want to make a connection, the best approach is to call the BBS operator and ask how you're supposed to make it.

By the way, BBSs aren't necessarily part of the Internet—although they can be. You do often see them being advertised slyly on the Internet, however. For example, some BBSs post graphics files and utilities in **newsgroups.** The BBS operators hope that once you see these newsgroups, you'll learn about their graphics files and utilities and you'll be willing to pay to **download** them.

Bit

Bit stands for binary digit. A bit is the smallest unit of computer data. Each bit represents a 1 or a 0. Bits are grouped in bunches of eight to form bytes, and bytes represent real information, such as letters and the digits 0 through 9. Modem transmission speeds, by the way, are measured in **bits per second** (bps).

SEE ALSO Baud; Bits Per Second; Kilobit; Kilobyte

Bitmap

A bitmap is simply a pattern of colored dots. On your screen, each colored dot is created as a pixel of light and is described by one or more **bits** (binary digits). This sounds like a bunch of gobbledygook, but if the colored dots are arranged in the right way, you get a picture such as the one shown below.

The reason I mention this is that you can **download,** or view, bitmap files in various file formats from newsgroups and **FTP** sites. Both **GIF** and **JPEG** formats are common, for example.

As a point of historical reference, I'll also mention that probably the best known bitmaps were those created in the late nineteenth century by the French impressionist Georges Seurat. In this case, however, the colored dots were created by brushstrokes on canvas rather than by pixels of light. And you thought this book was just about computers . . .

BITNET

BITNET is an acronym—almost. It stands for Because It's Time NETwork. BITNET started in the early 1980s and was mostly a university-oriented **network.** It networks mainly IBM and DEC mainframes and minicomputers. Usually used for mail and **file** transfers, BITNET's **LISTSERV**-based **mailing lists** are numerous and still very active. But today BITNET is diminishing in light of the Internet's popularity.

You don't really need to know anything about BITNET. But you sometimes hear the term being tossed around.

Bits Per Second

Your computer and all the other computers connected to the Internet use **bits** (binary digits) to store information. If you could look at your hard disk with a disk viewing utility (and they do exist), you would see a bunch of 1s and 0s. As a practical matter, you don't really need to know anything about bits (or bytes either). But they are sort of relevant because **modem** speeds are described in bits per second, or bps. A 2400bps modem can theoretically spew or swallow a stream of slightly more than a couple thousand 1s and 0s every second. A 14,400bps, or 14.4Kbps, modem can theoretically spew or swallow a stream of roughly fourteen thousand 1s and 0s every second. The faster the modem, the easier and faster it is to move data around the Internet. If you want to browse the **World Wide Web**, for example, you need a modem that goes at least 28.8Kbps.

SEE ALSO Baud

Bookmarks

Bookmarks are just uniform resource locators, or **URLs**, that you've told your web browser you want it to memorize. Some people call these memorized URLs bookmarks because that's what **Netscape Navigator** calls them. And some people call these memorized URLs **favorites** because that's what **Internet Explorer** calls them.

BPS SEE Bits Per Second

Bridge

You don't need to know the term *bridge* to use the Internet. But the term may come in handy at a cocktail party or a coffee klatsch. A bridge is a device that connects two **networks** so they appear to be a single, larger network.

SEE ALSO Gateway

Browser

A browser is a program that lets you look at **World Wide Web** documents. **Netscape Navigator** is a browser, for example. And so is **Internet Explorer,** which is what this book is mostly about. You now know everything you need to know to use the term *browser* with confidence. But since you're still reading, let me tell you a bit more. Most browsers let you browse, or view, both the graphics and text components of World Wide Web documents. But there are also browsers that let you look at just the text. For example, if you have a **shell account** and your **Internet service provider** supports the Lynx program, you can view just the text components of World Wide Web documents. (You might want to do this, for example, if your connection to the Internet is slow—say, less than 28.8Kbps—or if you're interested in only the text portions of the documents you're viewing.)

Newer browsers (including Internet Explorer) let you do more than just look at web pages. You can also use **FTP** sites, view **GIF** and **JPEG** graphics images, play videos and animations, interact with three-dimensional **VRML** worlds, and open text files.

Byte SEE Kilobyte

Cable Modem

Cable modems may just be the next big step in data transmission. A cable modem uses the existing cable company's cables—the same cables that bring premium channels, pay-per-view, home shopping channels, and dozens of other channels to your home television set. The sweet part of a cable modem is its speed. A cable modem can move data from the Internet to your **PC** at speeds of up to 30 megabits per second, and it can move data from your PC to the Internet at speeds of up to 1.5 megabits per second. To use a cable modem, your cable company needs to provide the service. If you're interested, call them and ask.

Cascading Style Sheets SEE CSS

CERT

CERT, another acronym, stands for Computer Emergency Response Team. Formed by the Advanced Research Projects Agency (ARPA) of the U.S. Department of Defense in 1988, CERT worries about the security of Internet **hosts.** So what does CERT do? CERT's main functions are to collect information about security breaches, coordinate responses to security breaches, and train the Internet community about security. It periodically issues advisories on security problems. You don't really need to know anything about CERT—just as you don't need to know anything about the U.S. Army's Delta Force Commandos. But it's reassuring to know that CERT (and the Delta Force Commandos) exist.

If you're really interested in what CERT does . . .

For recent advisories, check the newsgroup *comp.security.announce.* Archives of old advisories, as well as security-related programs and information, can be found at *ftp://ftp.cert.org.*

Certificate

A certificate is a digital signature that a software program on the Web carries with it to report who made the software and to indicate that the software hasn't been tampered with. The certificate ensures that the program won't transmit a virus to your computer or do something else harmful, such as erase your hard drive. An authority such as VeriSign *(http://www.verisign.com)* issues certificates to software developers who write safe code.

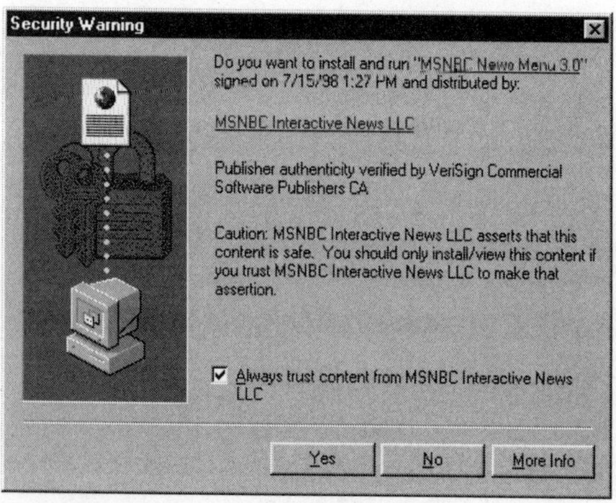

When you come across an Internet program to install on your computer, such as an ActiveX program, you will probably be presented with a certificate verifying the authenticity of the program. The certificate will tell you to install the program only if you trust the publisher to determine whether the program is safe or not. You can also choose to always trust the publisher by selecting the Always Trust Content From check box.

By the way, if you ever change your mind about a publisher that you told Internet Explorer to trust, that's okay. With Internet Explorer open, choose the Tools menu's Internet Options command. Click the Content tab, and then in the Certificates section, click Publishers. This will open a window with a list of the publishers that you previously chose to trust. Select any that you have changed your mind about, and then click Remove.

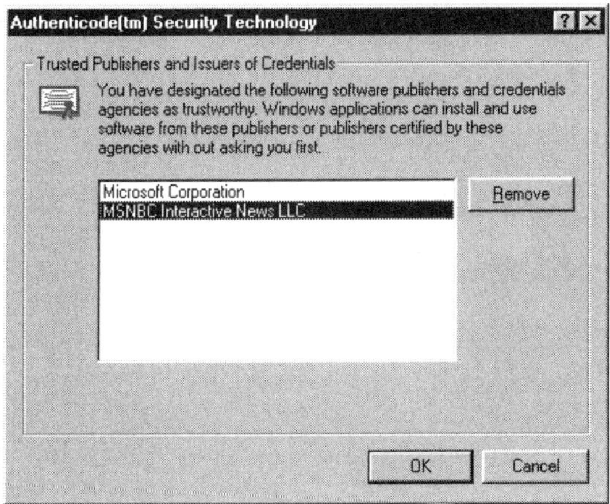

SEE ALSO Digital ID; Encryption

Channel

A channel is a web site that's been designed to deliver its information—its web page content—to your computer automatically. Channels then differ from regular web pages. As you probably know, with a regular web page, you and your web browser connect to a web server and then request a web page. (You typically make this request either by clicking a **hyperlink** or by entering a **URL** in the Address box of your web browser.) A channel, however, works differently. You tell the channel web site that you want to subscribe so that you get its information automatically on a regular basis. And then the channel web site does just that.

Subscribing to an Active Channel

To subscribe to a channel, start Internet Explorer and click the Favorites toolbar button to display the **Explorer bar.** Click Channels on the Explorer bar to display a list of categories. Pick a channel from one of the lists, or click the Microsoft Channel Guide button to display an up-to-date list of hundreds of channel web sites organized by topic. After finding the channel you want to subscribe to, click the channel's Add Active Channel button. Internet Explorer then asks whether you want the channel updated and if so, how often. (To make your choice, click a button.) And then you're finished.

Click this button to add an active channel to the Channels section of the Favorites menu.

Viewing an Active Channel

To view an active channel after you've subscribed to it, select the channel you've made active from the Channels section of the Favorites menu.

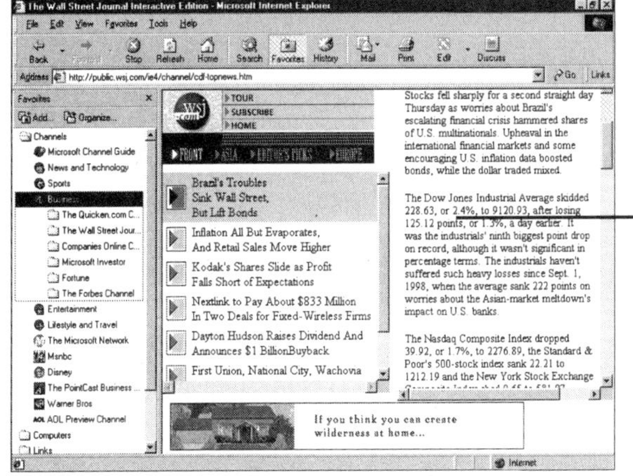

This is how an active channel's information looks. Basically, it's just a regular web page.

Chat

Chat, or more precisely Microsoft Chat, is an Internet **client** add-on that comes with Internet Explorer 5. Microsoft Chat lets you send and receive text messages with other users in real time. This means that you can read and respond to what other people type as they're typing. The participants in the chat need only be logged on at the same time and in the same place, called a chat room. To start Microsoft Chat, click the Start button and choose Programs. Then choose the Internet Explorer command to open the Internet Explorer submenu. Choose Microsoft Chat to display the Chat application window. In the dialog box that Chat displays, enter the name of the chat room you wish to participate in and the name of the server holding the chat. If you do not know any chat servers, your Internet service provider should be able to provide you with a list.

If you installed the standard version of Internet Explorer, you didn't install Chat. You need to install it from your CD or download it from the Web.

Circuit-Switching Network

The Internet is not a circuit-switching network. Let me explain. In a circuit-switching network, each network connection requires a dedicated line—a wire, a fiber-optic cable, even a satellite link or a microwave "link." The key feature of a circuit-switching network is that when one computer is talking to another computer, whatever the computers are using to talk to each other is used only for their connection. The most common circuit-switching network is the telephone system. When your computer (the one inside your head) is talking with another computer (perhaps the one inside your boss's head), the telephone line you're using is dedicated to your conversation and nothing else.

Now you might think that this has nothing to do with the Internet. And you're half right. But the reason I brought this up is that knowing what a circuit-switching network is helps you better understand what a packet-switching network is, which is what the Internet uses.

Client

When you're talking about the Internet, a client is a software program running on your personal computer that lets you use the Internet. Windows itself comes with several Internet clients, including **FTP**, **ping**, and **telnet**. And, interestingly, Internet Explorer 5 doesn't just supply the **Internet Explorer** web browser client but also several other clients, including Microsoft Outlook Express (an e-mail client) and Microsoft Chat (an online chat, or IRC, client). Client software programs work with server software programs that run on the computers you connect to.

SEE ALSO **Server**

Connections

You can connect to the Internet in several different ways. You can connect by way of a shell account from your work or school. With a shell account, you use a communications application such as HyperTerminal to connect to a server and you navigate the Internet textually using UNIX commands.

This Pocket Guide, however, assumes that you're connecting using Windows's **Dial-Up Networking** feature and **Internet Explorer.** With a Dial-Up Networking account from an Internet service provider you can browse graphical **World Wide Web** documents.

By the way, if you have scads of money, the time, and the technical expertise (or your employer does), you can connect your computer or **network** to the Internet permanently by using a **T1 transmission line.**

SEE ALSO FTP; PPP; SLIP; Telnet

Connection Wizard

Internet Explorer comes with a Connection Wizard that you can use to set up a new **Dial-Up Networking** connection even after you initially set up Internet Explorer. To use the Connection Wizard, click the Start button and then choose Programs, Internet Explorer, and Connection Wizard. By following the on-screen instructions, the wizard does everything necessary to connect your computer to the Internet. Once you run the wizard, you should be able to browse the **World Wide Web, FTP,** use **telnet,** send and receive **e-mail,** and view **newsgroups.**

Cookies

Cookies are files stored on your computer. Remote web **servers** you connect to create cookies to identify you and your web-browsing preferences. This all sounds a bit scary if you think about it very much, but cookies, used correctly, make your web browsing easier. If you frequently connect to a web site that requires a **username** and **password** (say, because it charges you money for viewing its content), this information can be stored in a cookie, which means you don't have to log on to the web site every time you visit it.

If you want to be warned before accepting cookies, choose the View menu's Internet Options command and click the Security tab. Choose the Custom security level, and then click Settings. Scroll down the list to the Miscellaneous category, and under the Cookies heading, select the Prompt Before Accepting Cookies check box and then click OK. Click OK again to exit the Internet Options dialog box.

CSS

CSS (Cascading Style Sheets) are a set of rules, usually embedded in a simple text file, that enable a web **browser** to display complex formatting in a **web page. Webmasters** use CSS to make multiple pages share the same formatting. Then when the webmaster wants to change the formatting for all the pages, instead of editing every single page, the webmaster simply edits the CSS file.

Cyberspace

Cyberspace is one of those loosely defined terms that—and this is very handy—most people use to mean whatever they want. If you put me on the spot and made me define it, however, I would say that cyberspace refers to the sum total of the activities and information on the world's computers, particularly the computers that are connected to the Internet.

Desktop

The desktop is the background screen that appears beneath application windows. In other words, the desktop is what you see after you start and log on to Windows. Internet Explorer lets you create an **Active Desktop,** which is a desktop to which you can add **desktop items,** which are basically web pages or portions of **web pages.**

This background is the desktop.

Desktop Items

Internet Explorer lets you add portions of **web pages** to your **desktop** if you've installed and turned on Internet Explorer's **Active Desktop** feature. These portions of web pages are called desktop items.

SEE ALSO Channel

Dial-Up Networking

To connect to the Internet using the **PPP** or **SLIP** protocol, you need to already have a PPP or SLIP **account** set up with an **Internet service provider.** You also need to use the Windows Dial-Up Networking feature. You use Dial-Up Networking to describe the connection (you do this only one time) and to make the PPP or SLIP connection (you do this every time you connect to the Internet).

Setting Up a PPP or SLIP Connection

Setting up a PPP or SLIP account is probably one of the most tedious and complicated tasks you'll ever do in Windows, at least as far as the Internet goes. You need to add the **TCP/IP** protocol, configure a **domain name** server, bind the Dial-Up Network adapter to the TCP/IP protocol, and then set up a Dial-Up Networking connection.

Fortunately, you usually shouldn't have to deal directly with the complexity of Dial-Up Networking. If you choose to use one of the Internet service providers that Internet Explorer knows about when you are installing Internet Explorer (and it probably knows about all of the large Internet service providers in your area), the setup program sets up the PPP or SLIP connection automatically. Alternatively, if you already have a Dial-Up Networking connection set up—say, you've already been using the Internet—you'll have the choice of using this PPP or SLIP connection.

If you have to do the actual work of describing exactly how the PPP connection or SLIP connection works, ask your Internet service provider for help and specific, step-by-step instructions.

continues

Dial-Up Networking *(continued)*

Making a PPP or SLIP Connection

You shouldn't have to do anything special to make a PPP or SLIP connection. If you start Internet Explorer, it checks to see whether a Dial-Up Networking connection is working. If a connection isn't working, Internet Explorer makes the PPP or SLIP connection, prompting for whatever information it needs. (If you need a **password** to connect to your Internet service provider, you'll see a dialog box that asks for this bit of information.)

SEE ALSO Authentication; Connection Wizard

Digital IDs

A digital ID is a tool you can use to sign your e-mail messages so that the people who receive your messages can be sure they actually came from you. A digital ID also allows you to encrypt your messages so that if a message is intercepted, the thief can't read the scrambled contents. To use a digital ID, you must sign up for one with a commercial firm that supplies and supports digital IDs. You can get more information about how this works by starting Outlook Express, choosing the Tools menu's Options command, clicking the Security tab, and then clicking More Info.

SEE ALSO Certificate

DNS

A DNS, or Domain Name Server, is like a smart, electronic post office. Imagine if all you had to do whenever you wanted to send someone a letter was write the person's name on the outside of the envelope. Then down at the post office, some friendly postal worker looked up the address of the person and mailed the letter. Sounds nice, right? Well, that is basically what a DNS does. Because of DNSs, you can refer to a host by using its **host name.** A DNS then does the work of looking up the host's **IP address** for you.

For example, if you wanted to fiddle-faddle around with the host named *ftp.microsoft.com*, the **TCP/IP** application you're using would use a DNS to look up the correct IP address, which just happens to be 198.105.232.1. (Your machine or a machine you have access to must be configured to use a name **server** that performs the actual looking up.)

Document Cache

Web browsers such as **Internet Explorer** use something called a document cache, and it's important to understand what the document cache is and how it works. (Internet Explorer calls it the Temporary Internet Files folder.) The document cache stores copies of **World Wide Web** documents and images on your hard disk so that you don't always have to grab them from some distant World Wide Web **server** in order to view them. Therefore, the document cache also provides a history of the web pages and images you've visited and viewed.

Flushing Your Document Cache

To remove the documents and images stored in your document cache, follow these steps:

1. Start Internet Explorer, if necessary.
2. Choose the Tools menu's Internet Options command. Internet Explorer opens the Internet Options dialog box.
3. Click the General tab.

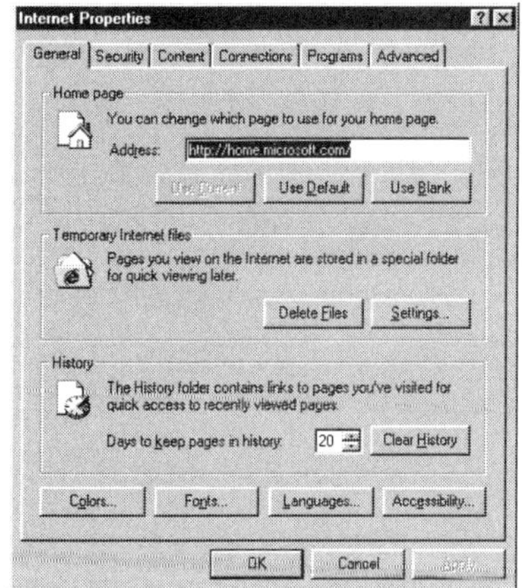

4. Click Delete Files to flush your document cache, the Temporary Internet Files folder. In the dialog box that appears, select the Delete All Offline Content check box to remove pages downloaded for offline browsing and then click OK.
5. Click Clear History to erase Internet Explorer's list of the **URLs** you've visited.

continues

Document Cache *(continued)*

Adjusting Your Document Cache

By default, Internet Explorer uses up to 10 percent of your hard disk for caching. (Internet Explorer may use a smaller percentage if your disk drive is very large.) You can change the size of the document cache by adjusting the percentage of your disk space used to store cached documents and images. To do this, follow these steps:

1 Start Internet Explorer.

2 Choose the Tools menu's Internet Options command.

3 Click Settings.

4 Select an option to specify when Internet Explorer should retrieve new copies of documents and images.

5 Move the Amount Of Disk Space To Use slider to adjust the size of the document cache.

If you don't want to use cached documents

If you don't want to use cached documents, click Refresh or choose the View menu's Refresh command. This tells Internet Explorer to grab a new copy of the document from its World Wide Web server rather than use the cached copy of the document on your hard disk.

Domain Names

The domain name identifies the organization that owns and operates an Internet network. The domain name has the format *organization.type*. The organization part is usually the name or acronym of the organization, for example, ***microsoft**.com* or ***mit**.edu*. And organizations have to register their domain with **InterNIC** or another equivalent domain registration service. The type part of the domain name can be one of the following from the table on the next page:

Type	What it means
.com	A company or commercial organization. For example, Microsoft's domain name is *microsoft.com.*
.edu	An educational institution. For example, the Massachusetts Institute of Technology's domain name is *mit.edu.*
.gov	A government site. For example, NASA's domain name is *nasa.gov.*
.mil	A military site. For example, the United States Air Force's domain name is *af.mil.*
.net	A gateway or other administrative host for a network. For example, UUNET's domain name is *uu.net.*
.org	An nonprofit organization that doesn't fit in the other classes of domain types. For example, the Electronic Frontier Foundation's domain name is *eff.org.*

Country types

The domain names of organizations located outside of the United States often use a two-letter country code either in place of or in addition to the three-letter organization-type codes listed above. For example, the two-letter country code for Australia is *au.* And the two-letter country code for Greece is *gr.* (For more examples of country names, see the list of Archie servers provided in the Archie A to Z entry.)

Domain Name Service SEE DNS

Downloading Files

In general, to download a file, all you need to do is click a **hyperlink** that points to the file. Note, too, that if you've already downloaded the file to view it with your browser, you don't need to download it a second time. To save a permanent copy of the file, choose the File menu's Save As command. If you're using an **online service** such as **America Online**, use whatever commands the online service's client software provides.

SEE ALSO Uploading Files

Dynamic HTML

Dynamic HTML (DHTML) is a set of web technologies that allow web pages to present moving, interactive graphics in a manner that minimizes download time. Netscape and Microsoft use different methods for implementing DHTML; web pages designed for Internet Explorer may appear differently when displayed in Navigator, and vice versa.

SEE ALSO HTML

E-Mail

E-mail, or electronic mail, is the Internet's most popular feature. If you have an e-mail client program and access to an e-mail service, you can send electronic mail to just about anyone whose e-mail address you know: the president of the United States (e-mail address: *president@whitehouse.gov*), me (e-mail address: *steve@stephenlnelson.com*), and even Mick Jagger. (I don't know Mr. Jagger's e-mail address.)

Because e-mail is such a popular Internet feature, Internet Explorer comes with an Internet mail client, **Outlook Express.** If your **Internet service provider** includes e-mail service, you can use Outlook Express to send and receive e-mail. For this reason, in the paragraphs that follow I'll describe how e-mail works with Outlook Express.

Configuring Outlook Express for E-Mail

If you use the **Connection Wizard** to set up a **Dial-Up Networking** connection with your Internet service provider—and this is how you should do this—you don't have to do anything special to configure Outlook Express or your computer for e-mail. The little work that needs to be done (principally identifying the mail **server** and setting up an Inbox folder for your messages) is carried out automatically. Therefore, if you have trouble getting Outlook Express to pass messages back and forth from your Internet service provider, contact your Internet service provider for assistance.

Creating an E-Mail Message

To create and send an e-mail message to someone, follow these steps:

1 Start Outlook Express.

2 Click New Mail. Outlook Express displays a new message form.

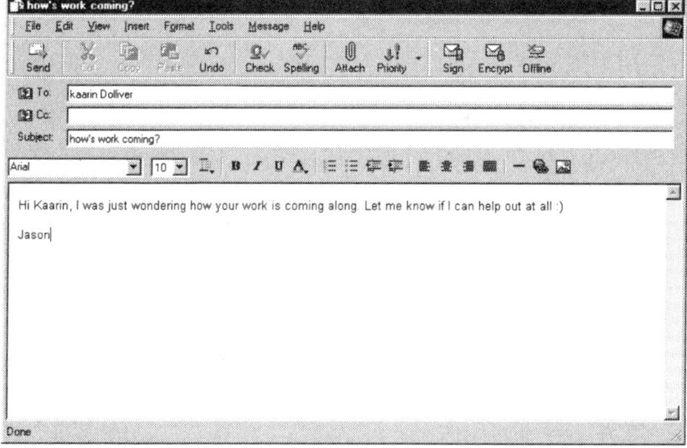

3 Enter the recipient's e-mail address in the To box. If you want to send the message to more than one person, separate the e-mail addresses with semicolons. If you want to use the Address Book to select your recipient(s), click the address card icon next to the To box. In the Select Recipients window, select the names of people to whom you want to send a message, and then click the To button. Click OK to return to your e-mail message.

4 Optionally, enter the e-mail address of whomever you want to receive a copy of the e-mail message in the Cc box, or click the address card icon next to the Cc box to use the Address Book to select the person's name.

5 If you want to send a copy of the message somewhat secretly, click the address card icon next to the To box, select the names of people to whom you'd like to secretly send the message, and then click Bcc. Click OK to return to the message form. Keep in mind that Bcc recipients will still show up in the header of the message, which some e-mail programs may display, so don't count on the secrecy for anything important.

continues

E-Mail *(continued)*

6 Enter a brief description of your message in the Subject box.

7 Use the main message text area to write your message.

8 To send your message when you're finished writing it, click the Send toolbar button. If you're already connected to the Internet, clicking Send sends the message to your Internet service provider's mail server (which then begins the process of delivering the message to the recipient). If you're not connected to the Internet—say, because you're working offline—clicking Send places the message in your Outbox.

Formatting e-mail messages

You can format your e-mail messages using the Formatting toolbar buttons that appear just above the message area. However, the people who receive your messages will only be able to see your formatting if their e-mail client accepts **HTML** or Rich Text Format messages.

Emptying Your Outbox

If you're not connected to the Internet when you click the Send toolbar button, Outlook Express places your outgoing e-mail message in its Outbox folder. To have Outlook Express pass all of the messages stored in the Outbox to your Internet service provider's mail server (so that the messages can be delivered), choose the Tools menu's Send And Receive command. If you have more than one e-mail account, choose the command that corresponds to your Internet service provider from the Send And Receive submenu. Outlook Express initiates a Dial-Up Networking connection, passes your outgoing e-mail messages to the Internet service provider's mail server, and then retrieves any incoming messages from the Internet service provider's mail server, too.

Retrieving Incoming E-Mail Messages

When you empty your Outbox folder following the instructions provided in the preceding paragraph, you also retrieve any incoming messages from the Internet service provider's mail server. Therefore, you retrieve incoming e-mail messages in the same manner that you deliver outgoing messages.

Reading E-Mail Messages You Receive

To read e-mail messages people have sent you, start Outlook Express and click the Inbox icon in the **folder pane** portion of the Outlook Express window. This tells Outlook Express to list any messages people have sent you in the message list pane of the Outlook Express window.

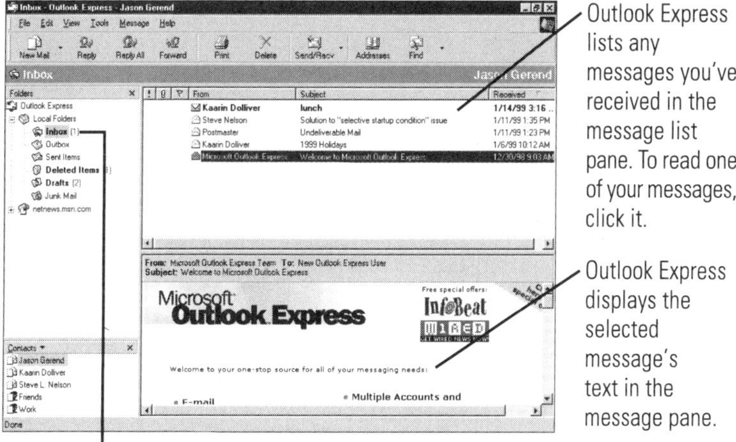

Outlook Express lists any messages you've received in the message list pane. To read one of your messages, click it.

Outlook Express displays the selected message's text in the message pane.

Click this icon to display the messages stored in your Inbox folder.

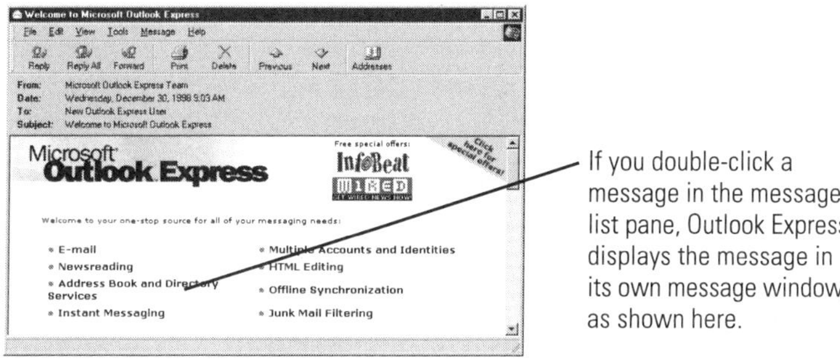

If you double-click a message in the message list pane, Outlook Express displays the message in its own message window, as shown here.

Forwarding an E-Mail Message

You can forward the open, or displayed, message to someone else by clicking the Forward toolbar button and then, when prompted, by specifying the e-mail address of the person to whom you want to forward the message.

Deleting an E-Mail Message

You can delete a displayed message by clicking the Delete toolbar button. When you delete a message, Outlook Express moves the message from the Inbox folder to the Deleted Items folder.

To view the items in the Deleted Items folder, click its icon. To delete a message that shows in the Deleted Items folder—this permanently deletes an item—select the item and then click the Delete toolbar button.

If you want to delete all the items shown in the Deleted Items folder, right-click the Deleted Items folder to display the shortcut menu. When Outlook Express displays the shortcut menu, choose the Empty "Deleted Item" Folder command.

continues

E-Mail *(continued)*

Replying to an E-Mail Message

You can reply to a message by clicking the Reply To Author toolbar button. (The Reply To Author toolbar button tells Outlook Express you want to send the message to the person who created the original message.) Or you can reply to a message by sending the reply to every recipient of the original message. To do this, click the Reply To All toolbar button.

When you reply to a message using either the Reply To Author or Reply To All toolbar button, Outlook Express opens a new message form, fills in the To box and Subject box for you, and copies the original message to the message text area. You can then add your reply to the message text area.

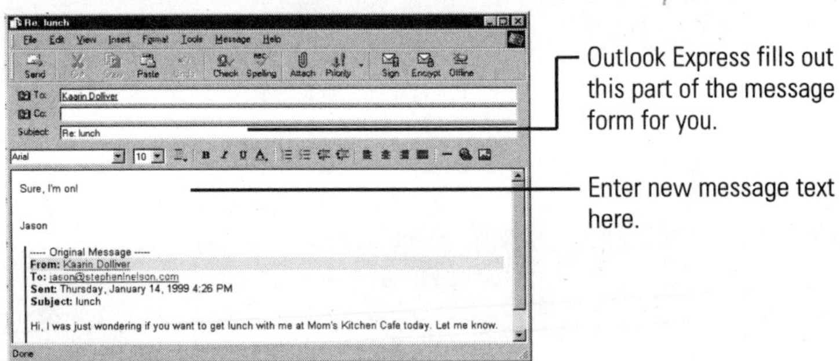

Sending a File with an E-Mail Message

Sending a file with an e-mail message is known as "attaching a file." To attach a file, create a message in the usual way. Then before you click the Send toolbar button, follow these steps:

1 Click the Attach File (the paperclip) toolbar button. Outlook Express displays the Insert Attachment dialog box.

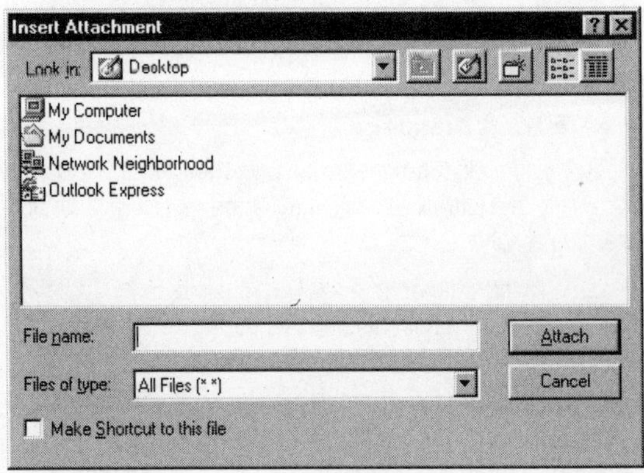

2 Use the Look In box or the Look In list box to find the folder that stores the file you want to attach.
3 When the Look In list box shows the file you want to attach, click it to select it. (After you do this, the File Name box will identify the file.)
4 Verify that the Make Shortcut To This File check box isn't cleared.
5 Click Attach to attach the file to the message.

After you attach the file to the message, you send the message in the usual way. For example, click the Send toolbar button to place the message in your Outbox folder. Later, to deliver the messages in your Outbox folder to your Internet service provider's mail server, click the Send And Receive toolbar button.

SEE ALSO Digital ID; Encoded Files; Encryption; Groups

More about e-mail attachments

E-mail messages usually include just text. But they can also include binary files—such as graphics images and programs. Almost every computer user has had problems with binary e-mail attachments at one point or another. This is because the e-mail server and client programs for both the message sender and the message receiver need to recognize the same protocol. The problem is that they often don't. For instance, if someone sends you a **MIME** attachment and your Internet service provider's server or e-mail client doesn't support the MIME protocol, the attachment shows up on your screen as a bunch of indecipherable garbage. To decode this mess, you need to use a program like **WinZip** or Wincode. Just for your information, Outlook Express recognizes both MIME and **uuencode.** Most Internet service providers support MIME these days, but you might want to ask your provider to be on the safe side.

E-Mail Address

An e-mail address is what you use to address an **e-mail** message. An e-mail address is typically composed of a person's **username** and the **domain name** of their **Internet service provider.** For example, my username is *steve* and my domain name is *stephenlnelson.com.* My e-mail address is *steve@stephenlnelson.com.*

You don't have to work with e-mail addresses if you don't want to, however. You can use the **Address Book** to make a list of people's names and e-mail addresses. And if you do record someone's name and e-mail address in your Address Book, all you need to do to address a message is to type in the person's name. Outlook Express grabs the person's e-mail address from your Address Book when it's time to actually send the message.

continues

E-Mail Address *(continued)*

Before we wrap up this discussion of e-mail addresses, let me mention that some people call e-mail addresses by other names. Some people call them e-mail names. And some people call them e-mail aliases.

E-Mail Lists SEE Mailing Lists

E-Mail Name SEE E-Mail Address

Emoticons SEE Smileys

Encoded Files

Here's one of the weird aspects of Internet **newsgroups:** You can't post binary **files,** such as **bitmap** images or programs. You can post only text. If you know much about Internet newsgroups, however, you're shaking your head now. You already know that bitmap images and programs are two of the items that people post most often.

So what gives? Well, here's the weirdness: To post a binary file—such as a picture or program—the poster first turns the binary file into a text file. Binary-to-text conversion is called encoding, or uuencoding. When someone wants to download an encoded binary file, they need to turn the text file back into a binary file. Text-to-binary conversion is called decoding, or unencoding. Fortunately, you don't need to do anything special to encode or decode binary files. Outlook Express automatically encodes binary files before you post them to newsgroups. And it automatically decodes any binary files you retrieve from newsgroups.

SEE ALSO MIME; Uuencode

Encryption

When you encrypt something—like an e-mail message—it just means that you scramble the information so that it can't be read by anyone who doesn't know how to unscramble it. When the recipient gets your e-mail message, he or she decrypts, or unscrambles, it in order to read it.

Mechanically, encryption is pretty simple. Let's take the following message as an example:

```
I'm dating Beth's mother but don't tell Beth!
```

If I create a simple little code that, for example, substitutes the number *2* for the letter *b*, fills spaces with the letter *x*, and substitutes the dollar sign for the letter *t*, the preceding message gets encrypted into this:

```
I'mxda$ingx2e$h'sxmo$herx2u$xdon'$x$ellx2e$h!
```

See how even a simple code makes a message pretty illegible? If Beth gets or intercepts this message, she probably wouldn't stumble onto my secret. But if my intended recipient knows the encryption scheme and can apply it backwards, he or she can easily decrypt and then read my message.

Anyone who really wanted to could probably figure out my simple code in relatively short order. But with a computer you can create and use wickedly complex encryption rules. In fact, with a computer's help, you can create and use encryption rules that are practically unbreakable.

So how does all of this apply to the Internet? While encryption may seem like a subject of interest to only the paranoid and conspiracy theorists, actually it's not. Encryption is necessary for the Internet to become a truly commercial network. You wouldn't want to send your credit card number without encryption, for example. Without encryption, some miscreant might intercept your credit card number and charge a trip to Acapulco.

SEE ALSO Certificate; Digital ID; PGP; ROT13

Escape Characters

If you connect to another Internet host—perhaps you've just **telnetted** to a host—you need a way to disconnect when you're finished. The way you disconnect is by pressing an escape character. The escape character is probably a two-character key sequence that you type to signal you want to disconnect.

continues

Escape Characters *(continued)*

When you connect to the U.S. Library of Congress's telnet site, for example, you're told, among other things, that the escape character is ^]. The caret symbol (^) signifies the Ctrl key. So to disconnect from the Library of Congress's telnet site, you press Ctrl+].

Typically, you get a lot of information when you first connect to a host, and buried in that information is the escape character. Be sure to write it down. Or failing that, try some of the more common escape sequences—such as Ctrl+] or Ctrl+C.

Want to telnet to the Library of Congress?

To telnet to the Library of Congress, you just need to enter the full uniform resource locator **(URL)** for the Library of Congress's telnet site in the Internet Explorer Address box. The full URL is *telnet://locis.loc.gov.* When you enter the telnet URL, Internet Explorer starts the Windows telnet client, which is what you'll use to work with the Library of Congress web site. By the way, once you connect to the Library of Congress or to any other telnet site, you use the site's menus to navigate and use the system.

Ethernet

Ethernet is a hardware standard for **LANs** developed by Xerox. It is one of the most popular standards. Ethernet can transfer data at speeds up to 10Mbps, or 100Mbps for Fast Ethernet. So that's pretty cool. (You do need to have an Ethernet adapter for your PC to connect to an Ethernet-based LAN.) This digression into network topology may seem irrelevant to a discussion of the Internet. But it is important to note that because Ethernet is so much faster than most of the connections the Internet uses, many of the things that people do on the Internet work even better on an **intranet** running a company's LAN.

Let me see if there's anything else I can say about Ethernet . . . as long as we're on the subject, I may as well tell you that there are three ways to make the actual connection based on the adapter and network: thin Ethernet cable using a BNC connector, twisted pair or 10BASE-T cable using an RJ-45 connector, and Thick Ethernet cable using an AUI connector.

SEE ALSO Bits Per Second

Exchange

Microsoft Exchange is more a set of technologies and products than it is a single software program. If you work at a large company with internal e-mail, you probably access an Exchange Server for your company e-mail, and you may be using an Exchange client to do this. Outlook Express doesn't support Exchange Server, so if you need access to an Exchange Server, you'll need to use either the Exchange client built into Windows or Microsoft Outlook.

Explorer Bar

The Explorer bar is a portion on the left side of the Internet Explorer window that shows a list of **hyperlinks** you can click. In the right portion of the window, Internet Explorer shows the active **web page.** By clicking the hyperlinks in the Explorer bar, you change the web page shown in the right portion of the Internet Explorer window.

To display the Explorer bar, choose the View menu's Explorer bar command and then choose what you'd like to display by clicking the Search, Favorites or History commands. You can also display the Explorer bar by clicking the Search, **Favorites,** or **History** toolbar buttons. After Internet Explorer displays the Explorer bar, click some of the hyperlinks to see how the open web page changes.

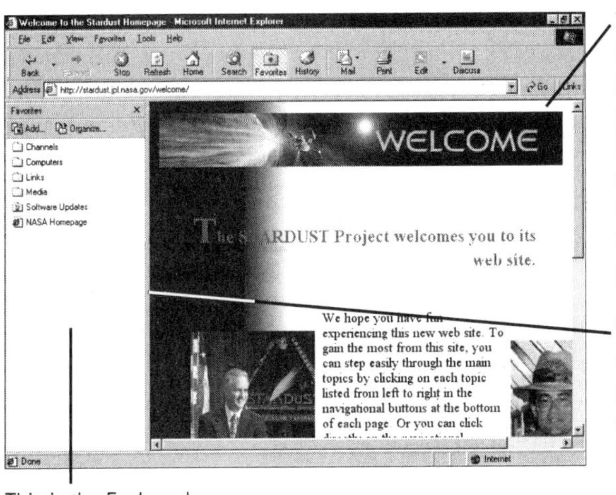

When you click a hyperlink in the Explorer bar, this portion of the Internet Explorer window shows the web page that the hyperlink points to.

You can change the size of the Explorer bar by dragging this border.

This is the Explorer bar.

FAQ

FAQ is an acronym for Frequently Asked Questions. A FAQ is a compilation of questions and answers posted often on **newsgroups** and **mailing lists.** FAQs do a couple of things. They give you a feel for what a newsgroup or mailing list is about, and they keep questions that have already been answered many times from appearing yet again.

You probably should read the FAQ for a newsgroup or mailing list you're interested in. Unless you're someone who enjoys being the subject of nasty criticism and endless **flames,** you should definitely check a group's FAQ before you post.

Just the FAQs, ma'am

FAQs are posted regularly in newsgroups as well as on *news://news.answers.* Archives of almost all FAQs can be found at *ftp://rtfm.mit.edu/pub/usenet.* A good search form can be found at *http://www.cis.ohio-state.edu/hypertext/faq/usenet/top.html.*

SEE ALSO Netiquette

Favorites

Favorites is the name of a folder that lists **web pages** you've said are so cool that you want Internet Explorer to memorize their uniform resource locators (**URLs**). You can guess why Internet Explorer lets you do this. By memorizing a URL, you don't have to remember some lengthy, complicated URL when you want to visit the web site again.

Adding an Item to Your Favorites List

To add the current web page to your favorites list, choose the Favorites menu's Add To Favorites command. When Internet Explorer displays the Add Favorite dialog box, name the favorite and click OK.

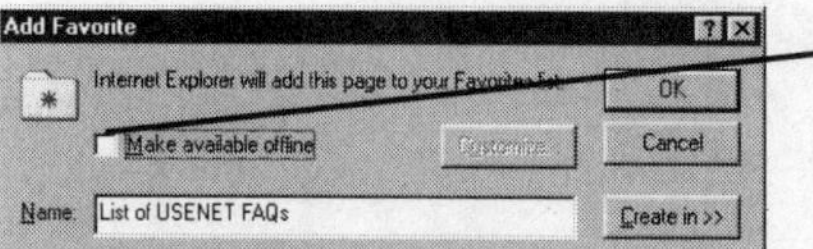

If you want Internet Explorer to automatically download updates to this web page, select the Make Available Offline check box.

Internet Explorer displays this dialog box after you click Create In.

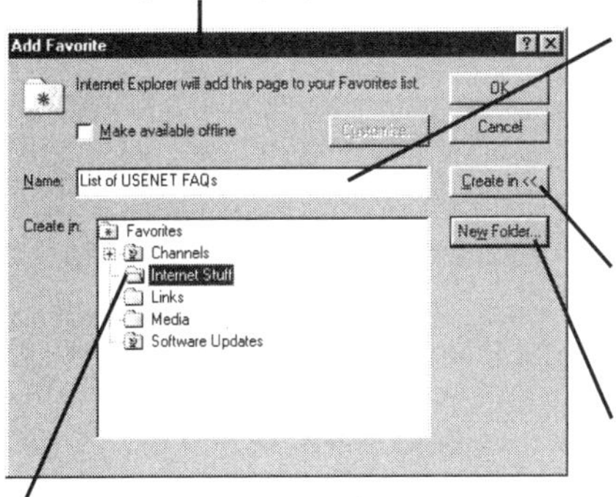

Internet Explorer suggests you use the web page name to identify the favorite, but you'll sometimes want to change this to something more descriptive.

If you want to store the favorite in one of the Favorite folder's subfolders, click Create In.

Click New Folder to create a new subfolder.

Double-click the subfolder you want to store the favorite in.

Visiting a Favorite Web Page

To visit a favorite web page, choose from the Favorites menu commands or click the Favorites toolbar button.

If you stored the favorite web page's URL in the Favorites folder, choose the web page from the Favorites menu.

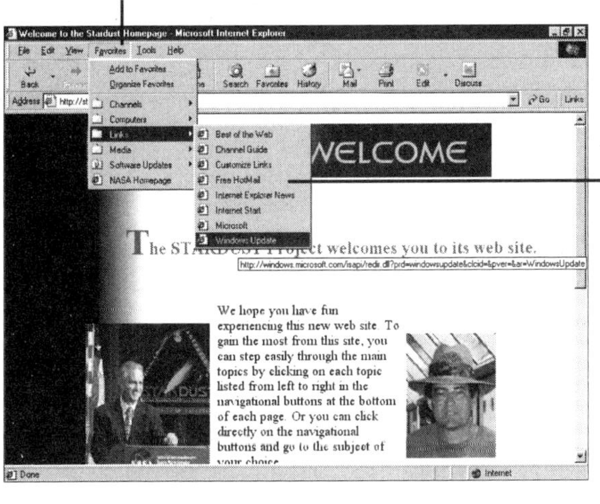

If you stored the favorite web page in a subfolder of the Favorites folder, click the subfolder and then choose the web page from the subfolder.

Organizing Your Favorites

After a while, you'll probably find that all of those favorites you've been storing has made your Favorites folder somewhat cluttered. Time for some housekeeping. To clean up your Favorites folder, choose the Favorites menu's Organize Favorites command. Use the Organize Favorites window to rearrange your favorites to better suit your needs.

continues

Favorites *(continued)*

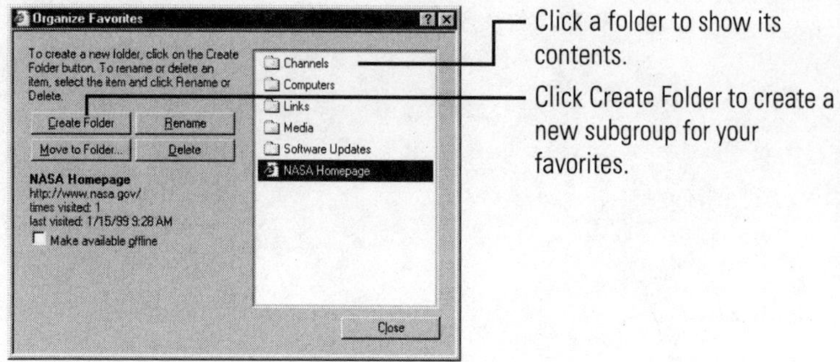

Importing and exporting favorites

To import or export favorites, choose the File menu's Import And Export command and then follow the instructions provided.

File

When you work with computers, you work with files. Data gets stored in files. Applications, or programs, are stored in files. When you begin work, you open a file. When you're finished, you save and close the file.

One of the main tasks the Internet performs, of course, is moving these files around. And, in fact, there's a protocol you'll probably work with that was created for the express purpose of moving files between Internet hosts: **FTP.**

File Extensions

Windows appends a three-letter file extension at the end of filenames to identify the file type. Because Windows does this, many of the files you download from the Internet also use a file extension to identify the file type.

What's more, because so many Internet users are also Windows users, it's considered good manners to **upload** files that follow the Windows file-naming conventions and use the three-letter file extension. Just so you know what some of the file extensions identify, I've listed the common ones in the table on the next page:

File extension	Type of file
ARC	A compressed file that's been scrunched with the archive utility.
AVI	A video file that uses the Microsoft Audio Video Interleaved, or AVI, file format.
EXE	A program, or executable, file.
GIF	A **bitmap** file that uses the Graphics Interchange Format, or **GIF**.
JPG	A bitmap file that uses the Joint Photographic Experts Group, or **JPEG,** format.
MPG	A video that uses the Moving Pictures Experts Group, or **MPEG,** format.
TXT	A text file.
UUE	A binary file—such as a program or bitmap file—that's been turned into text using a uuencode utility. To turn this file back into a program or bitmap file, you'll need to decode, or unencode, it.
WAV	A sound file using the Microsoft WAV (for waveform) audio format.
ZIP	A file that's been compressed, or scrunched, using the **PKZIP** or **WinZip** utility.

Filenames

With the newest versions of Windows—which Internet Explorer uses—you don't really have to worry about file-naming rules. For all practical purposes, you can use as many characters as you want in a filename. But things are a bit different on the Internet. Because of the legacy of MS-DOS's file-naming limitations and conventions (MS-DOS limited filenames to eight characters), you should limit the names of the files you upload to eight characters. All numbers and letters that appear on your keyboard are okay to use in filenames. And so are many other characters. You shouldn't, however, use characters that MS-DOS expects to use in special ways on its command line. These forbidden characters include spaces, asterisks, and question marks.

continues

Filenames *(continued)*

Naming a file

You usually give a file its filename when you choose the application's File Save As command. For example, if you want to save a copy of the web page shown in the Internet Explorer window, choose the File menu's Save As command. The Save As dialog box includes a box you use to name the file.

File Pane

When you start **Windows Explorer,** Windows displays a document window that shows the stuff that's connected to your computer—including any **folders** and **files.** This window is split into two portions called panes.

Since the right pane is the only one that shows files, I call it the file pane.

SEE ALSO My Computer

Finger

People with **shell accounts** usually have a special command available, called finger. (To be precise, this command is actually a **client** that runs on the **Internet service provider's** computer.) Here's the scoop. If you know someone's **e-mail address** and the **domain name** of the host they use, you might be able to learn their true identity by "fingering" them. For example, say you've just gotten a message from someone named "nelson" at uxx.edu. Perhaps, before you reply, you want to learn a bit more about this person. So you finger them. To do this, type the command finger at the command prompt, followed by the person's e-mail address. For example, to learn the true identify of *nelson@uxx.edu,* you would type

```
finger nelson@uxx.edu
```

Assuming the host you've fingered responds (and it may not), what you'll see next is some information on the certain someone you fingered, such as that shown here:

```
[uxx.edu]
       Name:  Nelson, Peter C.
 Department:  Electrical Engineering
      Title:  Associate Professor
      Phone:  555-3210
        Fax:  555-1234
    Address:  3015 ERF
           :  Campus MC 154
  E-mail to:  Peter.C.Nelson@uxx.edu
ADN Account:  nelson@xxx.uxx.edu
```

Flame

A flame is an **e-mail** message that's mean and nasty. If you e-mail a message to me and say that I'm a complete moron, utterly incapable of constructing a sentence, for example, that's a flame. By the way, if I e-mail you back a message that says your mother wears army boots and your sister is ugly, what we've got going is a "flame war."

Flames, as you might guess, violate all the rules of Internet good manners and etiquette. But because some of the people out surfing the Internet have the maturity of grade schoolers, you'll see quite a few flames. On a philosophical note, I suspect that the anonymity of the Internet has something to do with this meanness. You can say something really mean and threatening on the Internet, but you don't have to see the person's face or run into them at the grocery store.

SEE ALSO Netiquette; Spam

Folder

Windows uses folders to organize your disks and the **files** they store. (Folders, by the way, are the same as MS-DOS's directories.) You can also organize the files in a folder by creating folders within a folder. Basically, folders work like the drawers in a filing cabinet. You can create folders and see how your disk is organized into folders by using **Windows Explorer**.

SEE ALSO Subfolder

Folder Pane

I use the term *folder pane* to refer to the left portion of the window that Windows Explorer displays to show you what's connected to your computer, how your disks' folders are organized, and which files are in the active folder.

Frame

A frame is an **HTML** command that lets the author of a web site specify different web pages to be loaded into different parts of a window. For example, it is common to have a table of contents web page loaded in one frame for quick navigation and a main page loaded in a larger frame next to it. Frames are a popular feature, but many developers shy away from their use because they display differently on different types of browsers.

Freenet

The term *freenet* refers to an Internet **host** that people can use for free and thereby connect to the Internet for free. Schools, community groups, and libraries are often providers of freenet sites. If you're interested in exploring this angle, you might want to make telephone calls to schools, community groups, and libraries in your town.

On the subject of freenet sites, the downtown public library where I live (Seattle) provides a freenet site, and it has become popular with a bunch of homeless men. These guys, who call themselves the "network geeks," spend time surfing the Internet from the library's freenet site. As one of the network geeks explained, "Hey, we're homeless, not stupid."

Free Speech

You bought this book to learn more about the mechanics of Internet Explorer and the technology of the Internet. I know that. But I want to digress for just a moment and talk about free speech and the Internet.

The Internet, as you might know, makes it possible to share one's thoughts and ideas with millions of people. While this power isn't all that remarkable—after all, television and some of the big newspapers do it on a daily basis—it is remarkable in that there's no obligatory censorship or filtering of the information.

Think about it for a minute. Nowhere else can someone share a thought or idea with millions of people freely, without the help of editors, journalists, and media executives. That's the "good news," so to speak. But there's a "bad news" element to this lack of informal censorship and filtering. And it's the flip side of the same coin. Someone—anyone with an Internet connection—can share a thought or idea with millions of people freely. And in any group of 20 million people, of course, you'll find a few goofballs, dingbats, and dirtbags.

I strongly believe the good news outweighs the bad news. But I need to warn you: because some editor or journalist isn't filtering information for you, you need to filter the information for yourself. And because the Internet community is culturally diverse, you will most assuredly find material you disagree with on any subject about which you feel strongly. Politics. Religion. Sexuality. Good grammar.

I'm not going to spend any more space on this. But I encourage you to respect and appreciate the enormous benefits of the Internet's contribution to free speech.

Bad news for filmmakers, novelists, and conspiracy theorists

Jeepers, because we're on the subject, I should also mention that this communication change is bad news for some filmmakers, novelists, and conspiracy theorists. A fundamental element of many thriller stories and conspiracy theories is a protagonist who has vital information but can't share it with anybody important. Note, however, that with the Internet, this idea is totally outdated. In fact, by my rough calculation, more than a few of Alfred Hitchcock's movies, some of Robert Ludlum's novels, and most conspiracy theories become impossibly farfetched in light of this radical change in communication. If you have hard evidence that some world leader is a criminal, for example, you can post the evidence to an Internet **newsgroup** today and probably topple a government tomorrow. If you discover a cheap, renewable, safe energy source some Friday afternoon, you can tell the world about it over the weekend, and no one—not even somebody or some organization with billions or trillions of dollars to lose—can stop you.

FrontPage Express

Microsoft FrontPage Express amounts to a "lite" version of Microsoft FrontPage Editor, which is part of the Microsoft FrontPage suite of web-publishing programs. What FrontPage Express lets you do is create **HTML** documents (without actually knowing HTML) so that you can publish them on the Internet or an **intranet.** If you're interested in becoming a **web publisher,** go ahead and experiment with FrontPage Express. If you're familiar with other Microsoft programs (and in particular Microsoft Word), you'll soon be creating attractive web pages.

FrontPage Server Extensions SEE Server Extensions

FTP

FTP is an acronym for file transfer protocol. FTP allows you to move **files** from one Internet **host** to another. In fact, some hosts are set up specifically so you can rummage around inside them and look for stuff to FTP back to your host. (Your host can be either your Internet service provider's computer or your own PC.) These hosts are called, not surprisingly, FTP sites. If any Joe or Jane can log on to an FTP site—and there are plenty of sites they can log on to—the FTP site is called an **anonymous FTP** site.

FTPing with Internet Explorer

Internet Explorer makes it very easy to move files from an FTP site to your computer. All you have to do is enter the FTP site's **URL** in the Address box. When you do, Internet Explorer displays the contents of the site's root directory, or root folder.

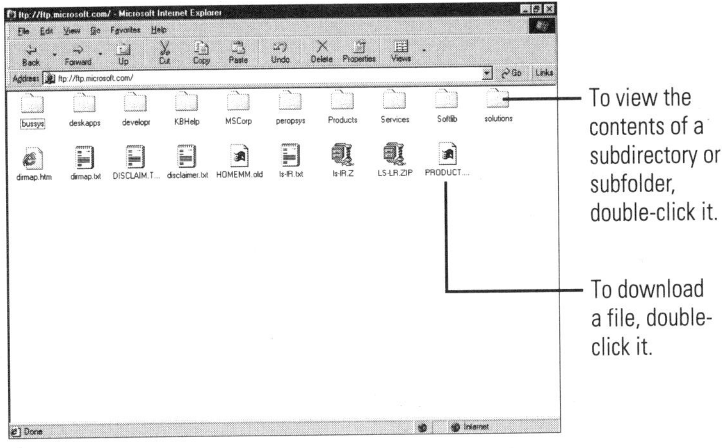

Logging on to a Password-Protected FTP Site

To log on so that you can upload files to a FTP site or use a FTP site other than anonymous FTP sites, follow these steps:

1 After going to your FTP site, choose the File menu's Login As command. Internet Explorer opens the FTP Login dialog box.

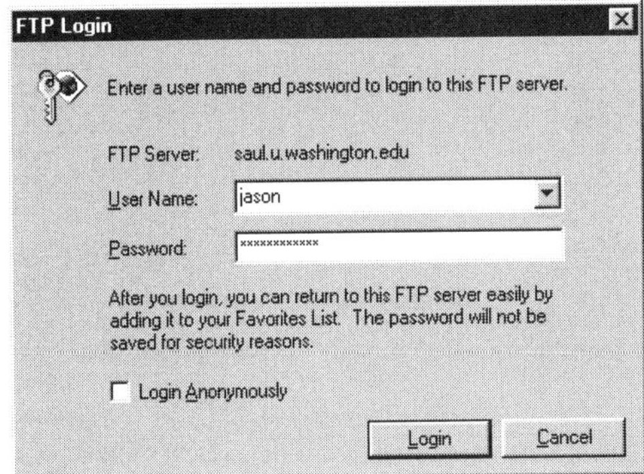

2 Enter your username and password.

3 Click Login.

continues

FTP *(continued)*

Uploading Files to an FTP Site

Uploading files to an FTP site is one way of getting files onto your web site if you have one. To upload files, follow these steps:

1 Enter the URL of the FTP site where you want to upload files.

2 Go to the directory to which you've been given permission to upload files. Most likely you'll be asked to log on at this point. If so, follow the instructions on logging on above.

3 Open Windows Explorer, and find the file or files you want to upload.

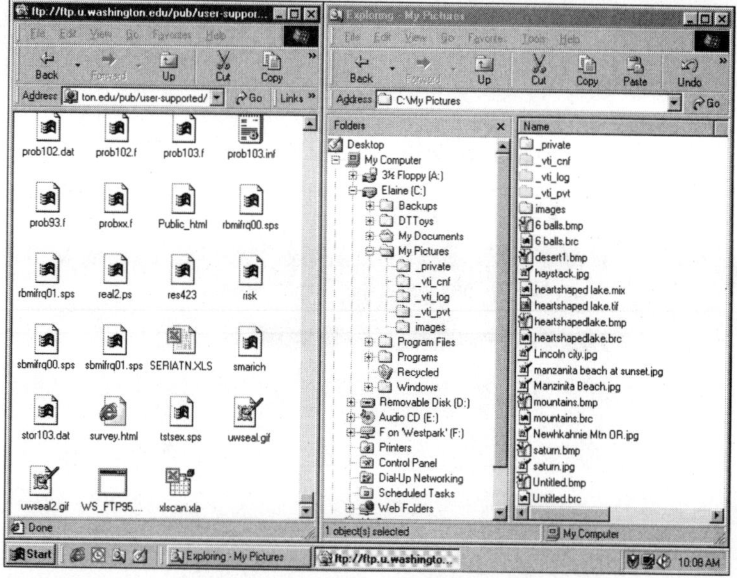

4 Drag the files from Windows Explorer to the FTP window where you want to upload them.

SEE ALSO **Anonymous FTP; Server Extensions; Web Publishing Wizard**

Full Screen

To see more of a web page on your screen at once, you can view the web page as a full screen. Choose the View menu's Fullscreen command to toggle in and out of the full screen mode.

Gateway

A gateway is just a computer that connects an **IP** network and a non-IP network. For example, **online services** such as **America Online,** CompuServe, The **Microsoft Network,** and Prodigy use gateways to connect to the Internet.

SEE ALSO Bridge

GIF

A GIF file is a bitmap file that uses the Graphics Interchange Format (GIF) file format. GIF files were the original graphics file format for the Web and historically have been the best supported by browsers. This is no longer the case, and thus the smaller and, therefore, quicker to download **JPEG** files are used preferentially over GIFs except for small icons and graphics, where GIFs still reign supreme. To look at a GIF file, you need to have a viewer such as **Internet Explorer.**

SEE ALSO Downloading Files

Gigabyte

A gigabyte is roughly 1000 **megabytes.** Since a megabyte is roughly 1000 **kilobytes,** it follows that a gigabyte is roughly 1,000,000 kilobytes (Kbps). That's big. Really big. For example, with a 28.8Kbps **modem** spewing data at a rate of 28.8Kbps, it would probably take three or four days to download a gigabyte of stuff.

Nits on bits

In the preceding paragraph, I gave only rough descriptions of the terms *megabyte* and *gigabyte.* To be painstakingly precise, a megabyte is actually 1024 kilobytes, and a gigabyte is actually 1024 megabytes, or 1,048,576 kilobytes.

Groups

Sometimes you'll want to send a single **e-mail** message to a number of people—maybe an invitation to friends about a barbeque you're planning or perhaps a weekly update to coworkers on your progress designing a car that runs on stale soda. These are the kinds of instances when having e-mail groups comes in handy. You can simply send a message to a group, such as Friends and Family, rather than adding individual e-mail addresses to the To field one at a time.

Setting Up E-Mail Groups in Outlook Express

To set up an e-mail group, start Outlook Express and then follow these steps:

1 Click the Addresses toolbar button to open the **Address Book.**

2 Click New, and then choose the New Group command from the submenu.

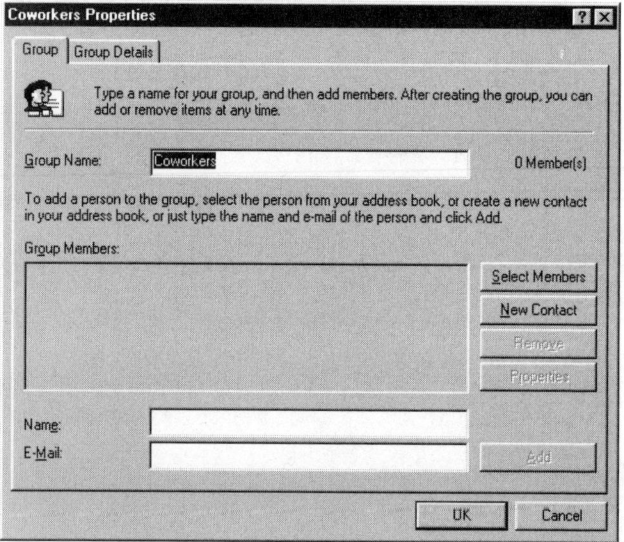

3 Type a descriptive name for the group in the Group Name text box.

4 Click the Group Details tab, and enter any additional information about the group.

5 Click the Group tab, click Select Members, and then choose whom you'd like to include in your group.

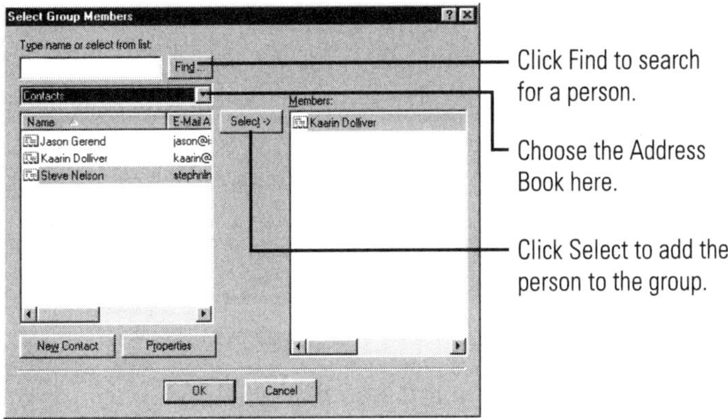

6 Click OK when you're finished.

Working with Groups

To e-mail everyone in a group, click the New Message toolbar button to open a new message, and then either type the name of the group in the To box or click the address card icon next to the To box and select the group from the Address Book. Write and send your message just like a normal message. But remember, everybody in your group will read the message.

Be careful who you put in what group

Groups are powerful things, but that power can backfire in a big way if you're not careful about adding people to your groups. For example, if you have a habit of writing personal updates that you send out to your Friends group, and in an update you complain about your boss, it wouldn't be so great if you accidentally added your boss to your Friends group.

Hackers

If you've read much of this book or you've surfed the Internet, you're not going to be surprised by what I say next: There's a dark side to the Internet. No, it's not that the technology is dehumanizing. Or that the Internet is a stepping stone on the path to some Orwellian future. The dark side stems from the hackers. "Who are the hackers?" you ask. (Hackers are also known by other names: "crackers" and "pirates.") Good question. These are the guys who break into host computers and then steal the information stored there or store their own information there. This maybe sounds innocuous, but it's really not. What they're sometimes stealing are things like people's credit card numbers. And what they're often storing are pornography or stolen software. I'm not sure that there's anything you (or I) can do about all this. But I think you should be aware that while most of the people you run into on the Internet are wonderful, there are a handful of dirtballs.

History

You can save yourself a lot of time if you pay a little attention to History. Internet Explorer keeps this in mind and has a special folder just to help you keep in touch with your history, and not surprisingly, it's called the History folder.

You use the History folder to find web pages you've recently visited because it's usually much quicker than trying to find them again. To open the History folder, click the History toolbar button. This opens the History folder in the **Explorer bar**.

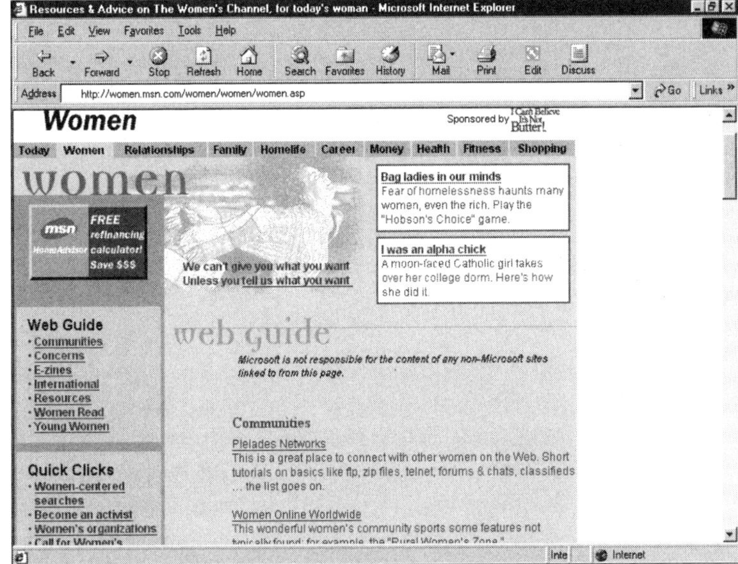

Open the folder corresponding to the time when you most recently visited the site. Internet Explorer displays a list of all the web sites you looked at in that time period. Browse through the list to find the page, and then click it to go back to it.

Home Page

The term *home page* is a bit nebulous. Sometimes people use the phrase to refer to the **start page** you see when you first start Internet Explorer. Other times, people use the term to refer to a personal web page (perhaps showing family pictures) that provides personal or business information. Usually, however, the term home page refers to the first page that you see when you visit a particular site.

SEE ALSO **FrontPage Express**

Host Computer

A host computer is just a computer that's connected to the Internet. For example, if you connect your PC to the Internet using a **PPP** connection, your PC temporarily becomes a host computer. Of course, any of the mainframe computers or minicomputers that you connect to are also host computers.

SEE ALSO **Server**

Host Names

Host names provide an easy way to identify hosts so you don't have to remember a host's **IP** number. Each host name can correspond to only one IP number. Host addresses have the format *hostname.domainname*—for example, *ftp.microsoft.com*. In this case, *ftp* is the host name and *microsoft.com* is the domain name. **DNS**, by the way, does the mapping of host names to IP numbers.

Hot Link SEE Hyperlink

HTML

The acronym HTML stands for Hypertext Markup Language. HTML is what you use to create **World Wide Web** documents. In fact, for this reason, the HTML acronym is often used as the last part of a World Wide Web document name—to identify what it is. (On PCs, World Wide Web documents use the **file extension** HTM for the same basic reason.) Do you need to know this? No, not really. The only time you'd even need to worry about or work with HTML is if you were creating your own World Wide Web documents.

SEE ALSO Active Server Pages; FrontPage Express

HTTP

This acronym stands for Hypertext Transfer Protocol. HTTP is the **protocol** that makes the **World Wide Web** possible. You may actually want to remember this acronym, because officially the **URL** for every World Wide Web site starts with it. For example, the URL for Microsoft Corporation's World Wide Web site looks like this:

```
http://www.microsoft.com
```

Note, however, that most web browsers, including Internet Explorer, don't require you to include the http:// part of a web page's URL. If you leave off this prefix, the web browser assumes it should use the prefix.

Hyperlink

Hyperlinks, also called hot links, hypertext links, links, and **anchors,** are those clickable blocks of text and clickable pictures you use to move to another web page. In other words, basically they're just uniform resource locators, or **URLs.** The URL doesn't show up of course. It's hidden. Instead you see text or a picture that (hopefully) describes or identifies what the URL points to.

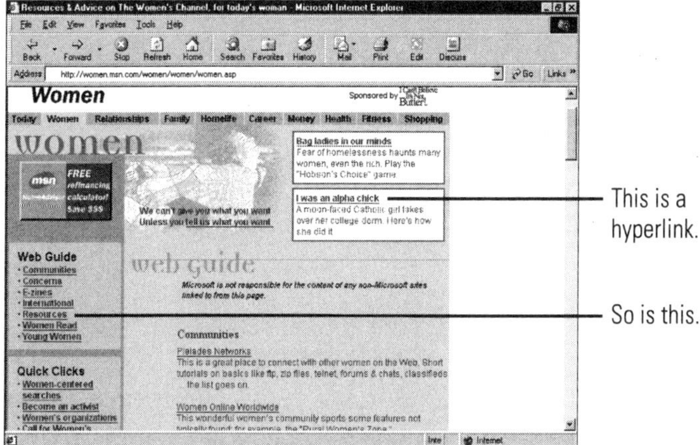

I should mention that not all hyperlinks point to web pages. Some start your e-mail client (probably Outlook Express) so that you can send a message to the person whose **e-mail address** is described in the hyperlink. Others launch another program such as a game or a spreadsheet. And some hyperlinks point to resources that aren't part of the World Wide Web but that are part of the Internet, such as **FTP** sites and **telnet** sites. When a hyperlink points to a resource that isn't part of the World Wide Web, clicking the hyperlink typically starts another Internet client.

HyperTerminal

HyperTerminal is Windows's powerful communications application. With it and a **modem**, you can connect your computer to another computer, to an electronic mail service, and to many electronic bulletin board systems, or BBSs. If you connect to the Internet using an Internet service provider and you're using a **shell account** and not making a **PPP** or **SLIP** connection, for example, you probably use HyperTerminal. Because this book doesn't discuss shell accounts and instead assumes you're making a **Dial-Up Networking** connection so that you can use Internet Explorer, I won't say more about HyperTerminal. But if you have questions, refer to the Windows documentation.

Inbox Assistant SEE Message Rules

Infoseek SEE Search Engine

Installing or Upgrading Internet Explorer

It's very easy to install Internet Explorer. But the way you install Internet Explorer and the options available differ depending on how you got the Internet Explorer program and any related programs.

Installing Internet Explorer from Microsoft's Web Site

If you have Windows 98, all you need to do to upgrade your version of Internet Explorer is launch the Windows Update tool. This tool will then walk you through downloading and installing the upgrade.

If you have Windows 95, you can download the latest version of Internet Explorer from Microsoft's web site: *www.microsoft.com/ie.*

Installing Internet Explorer from a CD

If you purchased or received Internet Explorer on a CD, you install Internet Explorer in the same way that you install other programs. To do this, follow these steps:

1. Click the Start button, click Settings, and then click Control Panel. Windows displays the Control Panel window.
2. Double-click the Add/Remove Programs tool.
3. Click Install, and then follow the on-screen instructions.

About Your Installation Options

If you have the complete Internet Explorer suite of programs (say, because you purchased Internet Explorer at the local software store), you will probably have a choice as to the Internet Explorer programs you can install. You can perform a "browser-only" installation, which installs only the Internet Explorer web browser client and some peripheral multimedia enhancements. You can perform a standard installation, which adds Outlook Express to the browser-only installation. And you can perform a full installation, which adds several other Internet clients (such as Microsoft Chat and Microsoft NetMeeting) as well as handy tools for web publishing (such as Microsoft FrontPage Express and Web Publishing Wizard) to the standard installation.

Integrated Service Digital Network SEE ISDN

Internet Address

When common folk like you and me use the term *Internet address,* we probably mean the URL of a particular web site, such as *www.microsoft.com.*

Some people, I should tell you, use the term Internet addresses to mean the same thing as **IP addresses,** or Internet Protocol addresses. IP addresses are the numbers that identify a specific host and domain. We could talk about IP addresses, but let's not. Unless you're setting up a **PPP** or **SLIP** connection manually, you'll never encounter them. And even then, you'll only have to noodle around with them once.

SEE ALSO DNS; E-Mail Address; Host Names

Internet Call SEE NetMeeting

Internet Explorer

Internet Explorer is Microsoft's web browser—and the principal subject of this Pocket Guide. As described in other A to Z entries, you use Internet Explorer for **web browsing,** to FTP, and a bunch of other cool things.

SEE ALSO Quick Reference: Internet Explorer Commands *and* Internet Explorer Toolbar Guide

Internet Service Provider

An Internet service provider, or ISP, is a company that lets you connect to its Internet host, usually for a fee. Once you're connected, your computer works either like a temporary Internet host or like a "dumb terminal" on which you can use the Internet by means of your connection to the provider's network. (When your computer works like a dumb terminal, you use your keyboard and your monitor, but it's really the other computer and its software that you're using.) People who talk about the Internet being an "information superhighway" like to say that Internet service providers are like on-ramps—they give you a way to get on the road.

One point that's a little bit confusing but important to understand is that you pay an Internet service provider merely to *access* the Internet. You're not paying anything to *use* the Internet. To go back to the on-ramps on the information superhighway analogy, Internet service providers set up tollbooths on the on-ramps that you must go through before you can get on the highway. But you actually use the highway for free.

Let me give you a few tips on picking an Internet service provider. First, check prices. You can pay anywhere from $10 to around $50 a month for an Internet service provider's service. (To keep your costs down, you'll probably want to choose a provider with local access numbers, or numbers you dial to connect to the Internet.) Second, you should verify that you'll be able to connect when you want. (You can test this just by trying to connect a few times before you actually sign up.) Finally, you probably want to verify that your Internet service provider gives you access to the **resources** that interest you. (Some Internet service providers don't give you access to the more controversial and sensational newsgroups, for example.) So ask about access to whatever you're interested in.

SEE ALSO Connections; Shell Account

Internet Society

The Internet Society is an international organization that coordinates the Internet and its technologies and applications. You can find more information about the Internet Society at the **World Wide Web** site *http://www.isoc.org.*

InterNIC

InterNIC refers to the Internet Network Information Center. The InterNIC stores information about the Internet. The InterNIC, for example, has information about all the various Internet standards that define and describe the **network** itself. The InterNIC also has information about a bunch of FTP sites. Its **URLs** are *rs.internic.net* and *www.internic.net* .

Intranet

An intranet is just an internal, private **network** that uses the TCP/IP protocol. (Many large organizations maintain intranets, for example.) You can use Internet Explorer to browse the **web pages** on an intranet in the exact same manner as you use it to browse web pages on the Internet.

IP

IP is an acronym for Internet Protocol. It is the network layer in the **TCP/IP** protocol. It ensures that **packets** get delivered to the correct destinations. IP is also the protocol after which the Internet was named.

IP Address

The IP address is the numeric address of a **host computer.** As a practical matter, you never need to worry about IP addresses unless you're involved in manually setting up a **PPP** or **SLIP** connection. Typically, the **Connection Wizard** automatically sets up your PPP or SLIP connection.

SEE ALSO DNS; E-Mail Address

ISDN

ISDN, the acronym for Integrated Services Digital Network, amounts to a super-fast telephone line you can use to connect to the Internet. While the fastest **modems** move data at 56.6 kilobits per second, for example, ISDN moves data at either 64 kilobits per second or 128 kilobits per second, depending on whether one or two channels, or phone lines, are being used. To make an ISDN connection, you need a special ISDN modem and ISDN service from your phone company. Your **Internet service provider** must also support ISDN connections.

SEE ALSO ADSL

ISP SEE Internet Service Provider

Java

Java is a programming language. This means that it actually isn't all that relevant to people who just want to use the Internet as a tool. However, you'll see the term used in quite a few places because Java lets **web publishers** write programs that can run on different computers. For example, a web publisher can write a Java program that calculates loan payments. (Perhaps the web publisher is a mortgage company using its web site to attract new borrowers.) And in this scenario, people viewing the web page with different computers can use the Java loan payment program to calculate their loan payments. Or at least they can as long as their web browsers know Java. If you're using a Windows personal computer and your web browser knows Java, you'll be able to run the program. If I'm using an Apple Macintosh and my web browser knows Java, I'll be able to run the program. If someone else is using a palmtop computer and a Java-aware web browser, they'll also be able to run the Java program.

JPEG

JPEG is a graphics file format. (The name is actually an acronym for Joint Photographic Experts Group.) Basically, the JPEG file format was created because people felt that other graphics file formats, including the ever-popular **GIF** format, were too big. JPEGs are much better at displaying high-resolution photos and graphics than are GIFs. And they're typically much smaller. You can identify JPEG files because they have the letters JPG as their **file extensions.**

Viewing JPEG Images

To view a JPEG file, you'll either need a browser with an internal JPEG viewer—like Internet Explorer—or an external viewer. Any viewer deserving of the name, however, will let you view JPEG files.

How JPEG Compression Works

To compress graphics images, the JPEG format simplifies an image by using fewer colors. And this is what reduces the image's size. While this of course does reduce the quality of the image—it usually doesn't reduce the quality of the image on your computer screen. What JPEG does is take two colors that are quite similar—say a very pale yellow-green and a very, very pale yellow-green—and make them both the same color (perhaps just a very pale yellow-green).

One challenge and potential problem with JPEG images, however, is that the image's creator typically gets to specify the degree of image compression that the final JPEG image uses. (The image creator does this in a graphics or illustration program.) If the image creator forces a lot of image compression, the color simplification can end up going too far. For example, the graphics program used to create the compressed JPEG image may be forced to treat colors that aren't all that similar—say a very pale yellow-green and a pale green—as equivalent, even though they won't be equivalent to most people's eyes. When this occurs, a JPEG image does suffer.

Kilobit

A kilobit is 1024 **bits.** You will find this information relevant because modem speeds are usually measured in kilobits. Don't confuse the terms *kilobit* and ***kilobyte.*** It takes eight kilobits to make one kilobyte.

Kilobyte

I know you didn't buy this book to learn about the guts of your computer. But since I've used the term *kilobyte* in a couple of places, I thought I should at least define it. A byte is an eight-digit string of 1s and 0s that your computer uses to represent a character. (These 1s and 0s are called **bits.**) This, for example, is a byte:

01010100

A kilobyte is roughly 1000 of these bytes. (Or to be excruciatingly precise, a kilobyte is exactly 1024 of these bytes.)

SEE ALSO Megabyte

LAN

LAN is an acronym for local area **network.** A LAN, for example, might connect all the computers in an office or in a building. You hear this term a lot in discussions about the Internet and about **intranets.** I don't know why. Whether an Internet **host** is on a LAN or a **WAN** makes little difference.

LISTSERV

LISTSERV is one of the more popular **mailing list** manager programs. (The other two mailing list programs you often see are Listproc and Majordomo.) So what does a mailing list manager program do? Simple. It adds users to and removes users from a mailing list. You can tell whether LISTSERV is the program used to maintain a particular mailing list because the **e-mail address** to which you send your subscription and termination requests will have LISTSERV in its name.

Log On

Logging on is what you do to connect to an Internet **host.** Specifically, logging on means to give your **username** and a **password** when you start using a computer.

Lurk

In a **newsgroup** or **mailing list,** lurking means to quietly observe. It means to read the posted messages and get a feel for what goes on and what doesn't before posting a message yourself. By lurking, you won't post a stupid message and get **flamed.**

Lycos SEE Search Engine

Mailing List

On the Internet, a mailing list is just a list of people who want to receive information via e-mail about a particular topic: BMW motorcycles, a particular television show, or some quirky author. If you want to receive information about a particular topic covered by a mailing list, you ask the mailing list administrator to add your name to the list. If you have something relevant to say about a topic, you can **e-mail** a message to the mailing list, and everybody on the list gets your message.

Configuring Outlook Express for Use with Mailing Lists

You don't do anything special to configure Outlook Express for use with mailing lists. If you can send and receive e-mail with Outlook Express, you're ready to begin using Internet mailing lists.

Finding the Mailing List You Want

Many, many mailing lists exist. So it can be a little difficult to find one that matches your interest. The phrase "needle in a haystack" comes to mind. You can, however, get a list of mailing lists from this **anonymous FTP** site: *ftp://rtfm.mit.edu/pub/usenet/news.answers/mail/mailing-lists*. What you want to do is get the **file** named part01 and at least a few of the other "part" files listed at this site. To start, for example, get part02 and part03, print these text files (you can use the Windows WordPad utility to do this), and read through the stuff. Take it from there.

You can also find a good list of mailing lists at the web site *http://www.neosoft.com/internet/paml/*.

If either of the preceding **URLs** don't work, use a **search engine** such as AltaVista to search on the terms "mailing list" or "publicly accessible mailing list."

continues

Mailing List *(continued)*

Subscribing to a Mailing List Administered by a Person

To get your name added to a mailing list, you need to know the e-mail address of the mailing list administrator. You also need the specific instructions for subscribing to the mailing list. These differ for each list, but you can get them from one of the lists of lists described in the previous paragraph.

Here's an example. If I wanted to subscribe to the mailing list *Birdfeeder*, a mailing list about birdhouses and bird feeders, I would send the following e-mail message:

```
To:         birdfeeder-request@userhome.com
Message:    SUBSCRIBE
```

A tip for new mailing list subscribers

You probably don't want to subscribe to a bunch of mailing lists right off the bat. Instead, subscribe to one. Or maybe two at the most. Otherwise, you'll find yourself overwhelmed with e-mail. And you don't want that to happen.

Unsubscribing from a Mailing List Administered by a Person

To have your name removed from a mailing list, just e-mail a message to the list administrator's address. Usually, when you first subscribe to the mailing list, you receive a welcome letter that includes instructions for unsubscribing to the list. It's a good idea to save this letter for future reference. Sometimes each edition of the mailing list includes instructions for unsubscribing as well.

A mailing list faux pas

When you send a subscription request, be sure you send your e-mail message to the mailing list administrator. You don't want to send the subscription request to the mailing list. Oh no. If you do, you'll be mailing your request to everyone on the list. The mailing list administrator's e-mail address is usually named *list-request*, where *list* is the name of the mailing list. Does that make sense? So if the mailing list name is *birdfeeder*, the mailing list administrator's address is probably *birdfeeder-request*.

Subscribing to a Mailing List Administered by a Program

One point that is sort of confusing about this whole mailing list business is that some mailing lists aren't administered by a person. Some of them are administered by programs such as Majordomo, **LISTSERV,** or Listproc. If the **username** that you e-mail your subscription request to is, for example, Majordomo, LISTSERV, or Listproc, you are actually sending your subscription request to the program that administers the mailing list. To learn the correct name of the program, site, and domain, you probably have to get the skinny from someone who's already subscribed. Or you have to get more detailed information about the mailing list. (For example, you could get the mailing list subscription information from the anonymous FTP site I described earlier.)

Once you get this information, you subscribe by sending the administrator an e-mail message. For example, to subscribe to the mailing list *bagpipe,* I would send my subscription request to *majordomo@piobaire.mines.uidaho.edu.* My e-mail message would look like this:

```
To:          majordomo@piobaire.mines.uidaho.edu
Message:     SUBSCRIBE BAGPIPE
```

Unsubscribing to a Mailing List Administered by a Program

To have your name removed from a mailing list administered by a program like Majordomo, LISTSERV, or Listproc, e-mail a message to the administrator and include the appropriate unsubscribe command. Which command you use to unsubscribe, however, depends on the mailing list administrator program. Check your first message from the mailing list for specific unsubscribing instructions.

For more help, request help

The mailing list administrator programs—Majordomo, LISTSERV, and Listproc—offer more commands than I've described here. You can usually get a list of the commands (with descriptions) that a mailing list administrator program uses by sending the one-word message "help" to the mailing list administrator.

SEE ALSO FTP; Outlook Express

Media Player

Microsoft Media Player lets you play active streaming format, or ASF, files as well as live ASF streams. In a nutshell, what all this means is that Internet Explorer can use Media Player to play multimedia clips you've grabbed off of the Internet or an **intranet.**

Megabyte

As you may already know, a byte is an eight-digit string of 1s and 0s that your computer uses to represent a character. This, for example, is the byte that represents the character A:

01010100.

A **kilobyte** is roughly 1000 of these bytes. (Or to be precise, a kilobyte is 1024 of these bytes.)

A megabyte is roughly 1,000,000 of these bytes. (Again, if you want to be precise, a megabyte is exactly 1,048,576 bytes.)

Another way to look at a megabyte is in terms of how long it takes you to **download** or **upload** a megabyte of stuff. With your **modem** passing data through at a rate of 28,800bps, or 28.8Kbps, it would take around 5 minutes to download or upload one megabyte of data.

Message Rules

Message Rules is a feature of **Outlook Express.** What it does is let you specify rules that Outlook Express should apply to messages appearing in one of your folders. For example, you can use Message Rules to automatically remove messages that use specified words in their subject descriptions. And you can use Message Rules to automatically forward, delete, or reply to messages that come from particular people.

Setting Up Message Rules

To set up Message Rules in Outlook Express, follow these steps:

1 Choose the Tools menu's Message Rules command, and then choose Mail from the submenu.

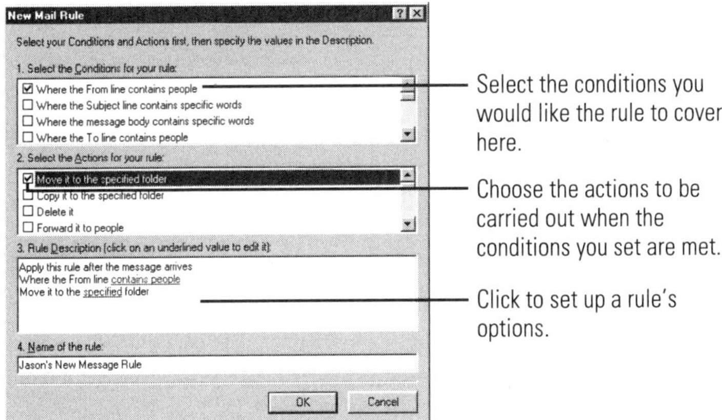

2 In the first list box, specify the conditions that need to be met for the rule to take action.

3 In the second list box, select what you would like done with any messages that meet the conditions you just set up.

4 In the third list box, click any underlined words to set the rule's options.

5 Type a name for the rule in the Name Of The Rule text box.

6 Click OK when you're finished to complete the rule.

7 Click Apply Now if you want to use the rule on messages already received.

8 Click OK to set the rule in motion, or clear the check box next to the rule to disable it, and then click OK.

SEE ALSO E-Mail

Microsoft Chat SEE Chat

Microsoft Exchange SEE Exchange

Microsoft FrontPage Express SEE FrontPage Express

Microsoft Media Player SEE Media Player

Microsoft NetMeeting SEE NetMeeting

Microsoft Network

Microsoft Network, or more precisely, The Microsoft Network, is the name of Microsoft's **online service.** I mention this here because The Microsoft Network provides an easy way to connect to the Internet. With the version of The Microsoft Network that's available as I'm writing this, you can browse the **World Wide Web** (including **FTP** sites), send and receive e-mail, participate in **mailing lists,** and read and post messages to **newsgroups.** To sign up for The Microsoft Network (or any other **Internet service provider**), use the **Connection Wizard** that comes with Internet Explorer.

Microsoft Outlook Express SEE Outlook Express

Microsoft Wallet SEE Wallet

MIME

MIME is an acronym for Multipurpose Internet Mail Extensions. MIME is a protocol that lets you attach binary **files**—like **JPEG** files, **GIF** files, **MPEG** files, and so on—to **e-mail** messages. As long as the people you send messages to also have e-mail readers that support the MIME protocol, they can extract and use the files you send them. For example, you could use MIME to attach a Microsoft Word for Windows document to an e-mail message. If the recipient's e-mail reader supports MIME, the recipient can extract the Word document from the e-mail message. If the recipient has a copy of Word for Windows, he or she can open and work with the document in Word.

Although MIME is really useful, not all e-mail clients and not all e-mail servers support it. In this case, you can still send binary files in e-mail, but you will need to use another tool called **uuencode.** You can also still receive binary files, but you will need to decode the attachments using a decoding utility.

Modem

A modem—the word means *modulator/demodulator*—is a hardware device for sending digital information like **files** and messages over telephone lines. To send this digital information, the modem converts computer data into sounds and sends the sounds over the telephone line to another modem and computer at the other end of the telephone line. To receive this digital information, the modem hears the sounds coming over the telephone line and converts the sounds back into digital code that a computer can read.

How fast a modem can send or receive data is measured in **bits per second,** or bps. Modems with higher bps rates can send and receive data faster. When you are shopping for a modem, buy a V.90 56Kbps model. They are pretty much the standard nowadays, so don't skimp and buy something less; you'll save money in the long run because you won't spend as much time using **online services,** which charge by the hour. Fast modems can download information quicker.

SEE ALSO **Baud; Downloading Files**

Moderator

A moderator is someone who decides which **articles** are posted to a **newsgroup** or which e-mail messages are sent to the people on a **mailing list.** A newsgroup or mailing list that has one of these characters is called, cleverly enough, a moderated newsgroup or a moderated mailing list.

For the readers or users of a newsgroup or mailing list, moderators are wonderful. They make sure that people stay on track. And they weed out the silly articles and messages that waste people's time and disk space. In fact, if I were to offer a single suggestion for making the best use of your time with things like newsgroups and mailing lists, I'd suggest that you stick to those with moderators.

Unfortunately, if you're trying to post to a newsgroup or send e-mail messages to a mailing list, moderators can be really frustrating. They might seem like censors. Sometimes they filter out the most cogent and poignant ideas. And they always take a while to review the articles and messages you want to post.

SEE ALSO **Netiquette**

MPEG

MPEG is a graphics file format for video, or movies. (The acronym stands for Moving Pictures Experts Group.) Like **JPEG,** MPEG was developed to provide a very efficient and compressed format for storing high-quality video. To view an MPEG file, you need an MPEG viewer.

Multitasking

Multitasking refers to the running of more than one application at the same time. You may not think you care about this, but actually you do. Because Windows lets you smoothly multitask, you can be working away with your word processor, for example, at the same time as Internet Explorer is slaving away to download a huge file. Windows automatically multitasks Windows-based applications. Whenever you or Windows opens more than one Windows-based application, you're multitasking. To switch between the applications you're running, just click application buttons on the Taskbar.

SEE ALSO Switching Tasks

My Computer

Internet Explorer lets you do more than just browse the World Wide Web. You can use Internet Explorer to also look at your local computer's disks, folders, and files. To use Internet Explorer in this way, start Internet Explorer and then choose the Go menu's My Computer command. When you do this, Internet Explorer displays the My Computer window.

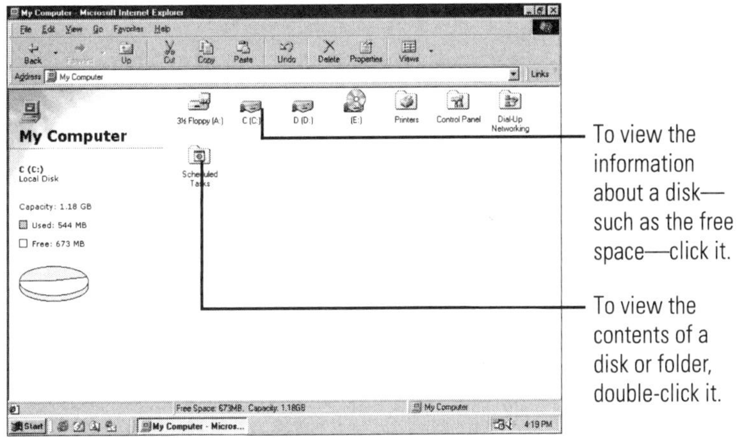

More about the Internet Explorer and the My Computer view

Almost everything you can do with **Windows Explorer** you can also do with My Computer. For example, you can open folders, programs, and documents; rename and delete folders and documents; and even access Control Panel tools. In fact, Windows Explorer and Internet Explorer are really one and the same, and both can do just about all the same things.

Name Server SEE DNS

Netiquette

Netiquette is the special word that's been coined to describe Internet etiquette. Fortunately, Internet etiquette—netiquette—isn't complicated.

On the Internet, you just have to be polite. If an organization lets you anonymously **telnet** or **FTP** to their host, follow any rules they suggest for usage. (Like hours the host can be accessed.) Don't flame people. Don't post articles that waste people's time to newsgroups (like a "Me, too!" message). Don't **spam.** Make sure you post articles to the correct newsgroup. If you have a question about what is and is not proper netiquette, **lurk** or look for a **FAQ.**

SEE ALSO RTFM; Shouting

NetMeeting

Microsoft NetMeeting is an Internet client that lets you communicate with other people over either the Internet or an **intranet.** Using NetMeeting, you can talk to other people, video-conference, share programs and documents, send and receive files, draw on a virtual whiteboard, and even **chat.** When you use NetMeeting to communicate with someone else, it's called an Internet Call.

Netscape Navigator

Netscape Navigator (or Communicator, which has Navigator bundled with some other programs) is another web **browser.** It competes with Microsoft's Internet Explorer. While you presumably use Internet Explorer as your web browser if you purchased or are reading this book, let me just say that most everything you read here about the Internet and **web browsing** applies with equal force to Netscape Navigator. And since version 4, Navigator has been available for free, too. It often makes sense to have both, just in case one works better than the other does in certain circumstances.

Network

A network is just a bunch of computers that are connected together. Windows 95 and Windows 98, for example, let you create what are called peer-to-peer networks as long as you've got **Ethernet** cards installed in the computers and the right kind of cabling to connect the Ethernet cards. But I'm getting off the track. The reason I mention this is because the Internet is really a network of networks. But one thing I probably should mention is that while all of the individual networks, or subnets, that make up the Internet are **TCP/IP** networks, the individual hosts use a bunch of different operating systems. Some of these hosts use Windows for their operating system. But other hosts use **UNIX,** Windows NT, and even DEC and IBM mainframe and minicomputer operating systems.

Newbie

A newbie is someone who's new to the neighborhood—the Internet neighborhood, that is. Everybody on the Internet was a newbie once, of course. But many experienced veterans of the Internet forget this. So newbies often get picked on. In fairness to the old-timers, newbies can become rather a nuisance on the Internet because many of them don't **lurk**, they ignore the **FAQs**, and they refuse to **RTFM.** Probably the best way to avoid this abuse is to be sensitive to the informal rules and protocols of the Internet, which will minimize mistakes on your part.

SEE ALSO Netiquette

Newsgroup

A newsgroup is basically an electronic corkboard where people post and read messages related to a particular topic or interest. For free. And with more than 10,000 active newsgroups, there's a newsgroup on just about every topic imaginable. In fact, I think it's fair to say that newsgroups are probably one of the three most popular **resources** available on the Internet. (**E-mail** and the **World Wide Web** are the other two.)

To write messages for and read messages on a newsgroup, you need a newsgroup reader. Because this book is about Internet Explorer, I'm going to assume that you'll use **Outlook Express** (which comes with Internet Explorer) as your newsgroup reader.

Configuring Outlook Express as Your Newsgroup Reader

You shouldn't need to do anything special to use Outlook Express as your newsgroup reader. Technically, the only real prerequisite to using Outlook Express as a newsgroup reader is that you need to tell Outlook Express the name of your Internet service provider's news NNTP server. But you shouldn't have to worry about this specification. The **Connection Wizard** does this for you. If you have problems performing any of the actions described in the paragraphs that follow, call your **Internet service provider** and ask for help.

continues

Newsgroup *(continued)*

Checking Out and Subscribing to Newsgroups

In order to read and post to newsgroups, you need to first download the list of newsgroups available on your Internet service provider's news server and then you need to find newsgroups that interest you. To do this, follow these steps:

1. Start Outlook Express.
2. In the folder pane, click your news account, and then click the Newsgroups toolbar button.

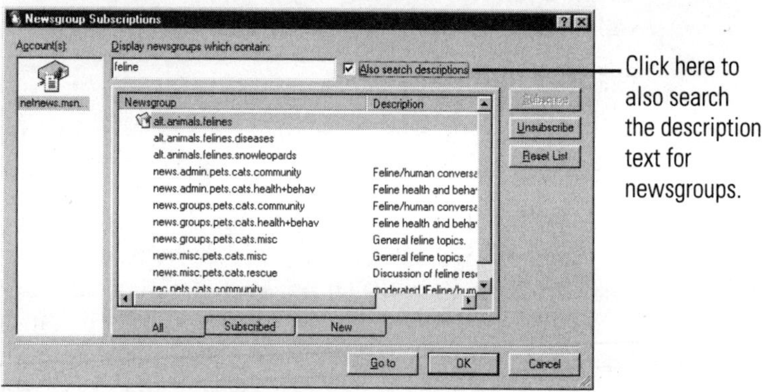

3. Click the All tab to display a list of the newsgroups maintained by your Internet service provider's news server. (If this is the first time you've displayed the All tab of the Newsgroups dialog box, you may have to wait while Outlook Express retrieves a list of newsgroups from the Internet service provider's news server.)
4. Enter a keyword in the text box to display all newsgroups that include that word, or alternately, scroll through the list of newsgroups until you find a newsgroup that you think might interest you.
5. Select the newsgroup, and click Go To if you want to preview the newsgroup. Click Subscribe to subscribe to the newsgroup. When you subscribe to a newsgroup, you add it to your list so that you can quickly access it, whereas if you preview the newsgroup, it disappears from your list as soon as you exit Outlook Express. (If you are working offline, choose the Tools menu's Synchronize Item Now command to connect and download the article headers.)

Unsubscribing from Newsgroups

You can unsubscribe from newsgroups you no longer want to browse. To unsubscribe, click your news server in the folder pane and click the Newsgroups toolbar button as described in the preceding paragraphs. Click the Subscribed tab at the bottom of the window, select the newsgroup from which you want to unsubscribe, and then click Unsubscribe.

Want to test out this posting business?

The busiest newsgroup you'll see is *alt.test*. It's the one you use to test whether your posting technique works. If you want to try out the steps I've described here, post to *alt.test*. To see if your message posted correctly, check that newsgroup in an hour or so. (Or check it tomorrow.) By the way, you'll get automatic **e-mail** responses from some of the **NNTP** sites that maintain the *alt.test* newsgroup. They send responses so you know your message got posted. If you don't want to see any of these responses, include the word "ignore" in your message header.

Reading Newsgroup Articles

After you have downloaded the article headers for a newsgroup, you can begin reading the individual articles. To do this, follow these steps:

1. Start Outlook Express.
2. Click the newsgroup you want to browse. Outlook Express retrieves a list of the articles posted to the newsgroup and displays a list in the right pane of the Outlook Express window.

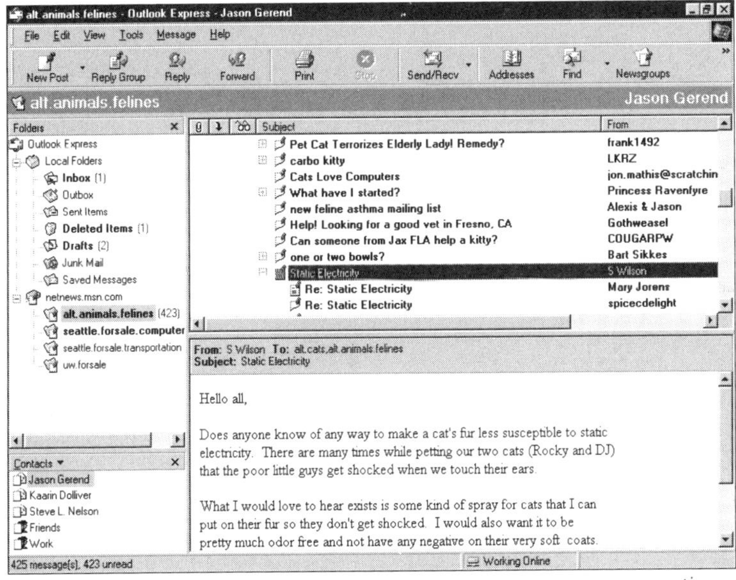

continues

Newsgroup *(continued)*

3 Click a message you want to browse. Outlook Express opens the message and displays it in the message area of the Outlook Express window.

4 If you want to see an article in its own window, double-click the article and Outlook Express displays the article in its own message window. When you finish reading the message, close the message window by clicking its Close box.

Moving to another article

To read the previous article, press the Up arrow key. To read the next message, press the Down arrow key.

Saving Attachments

If a newsgroup article includes a binary file attachment, you can save the attachment. (The attachment will show in the article either as an icon or, in the case of a graphics image, as a picture of the image itself.) To save the attachment to your hard disk, follow these steps:

1 Right-click the icon or the image.

2 Choose the shortcut menu's Save As command. (The exact name of this command depends on the type of attachment.) Outlook Express displays the Save Attachments dialog box.

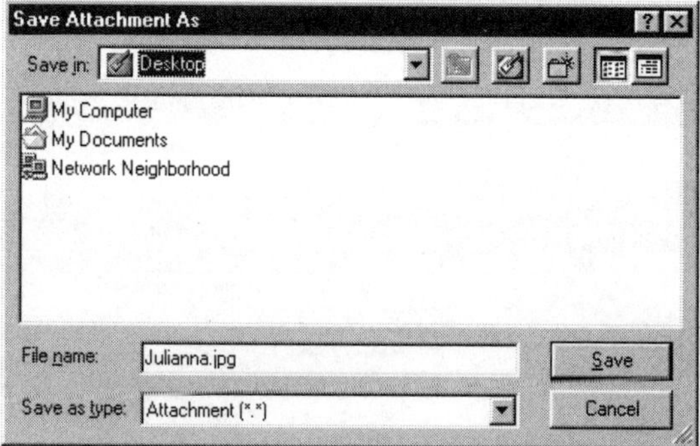

3 If the default location is the one you want for your file, click Save; otherwise, first double-click the folder you want to save in.

Saving Attachments That Are Split Among Multiple Messages

Because some newsgroup readers and servers limit article sizes, people commonly break large attachments into several small pieces and then post individual pieces in separate messages. A 1MB attachment, for example, might be broken into five smaller pieces posted in five individual messages. (To identify these multipart attachments, people use message subject descriptions such as "File 1/5," "File 2/5," " File 3/5," and so on.) Outlook Express lets you easily download these message parts and combine the attachments. To download an attachment stored as several pieces across multiple messages, follow these steps:

1. Select the messages that hold the attachments. (You can do this by holding down the Ctrl key and then clicking each message.)
2. Right-click the selection.
3. Choose the shortcut menu's Combine And Decode command. Outlook Express displays the Order For Decoding dialog box.
4. Verify that the messages appear in the right order—the first part first, the second part second, and so on. If the messages don't appear in the correct order, use the Move Up and Move Down buttons to arrange them correctly.
5. Click OK.

Posting Text-Only Articles

To post an article to a newsgroup, follow these steps:

1. Start Outlook Express.
2. Click the newsgroup to which you want to post an article.
3. Click the New Message toolbar button. Outlook Express displays a new message form.

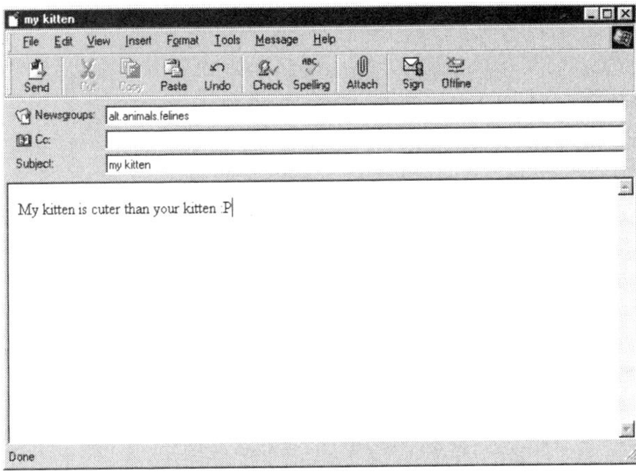

4. Create your article.
5. To post the article, click the Send toolbar button. Outlook Express posts the article to the news server. (Note, however, that it may take a while for the news server to make the message available.)

continues

Newsgroup *(continued)*

Private replies

You can reply privately to the person who posted an article rather than to the newsgroup. To reply to an article privately, select the article and then click the Reply toolbar button. To reply to the newsgroup, click the Reply Group toolbar button. When Outlook Express displays a new message form, enter your message and click the Send toolbar button.

Posting Articles with Attachments

You post articles with attachments in almost the same manner as you post articles without attachments. To post an article with an attachment to a newsgroup, follow these steps:

1. Start Outlook Express.
2. Click the newsgroup to which you want to post an article.
3. Click the New Message toolbar button. Outlook Express displays a new message form.
4. Create your article.
5. Click the Attach File (the paperclip) icon on the toolbar. Outlook Express displays the Insert Attachment dialog box.
6. Identify the attachment.

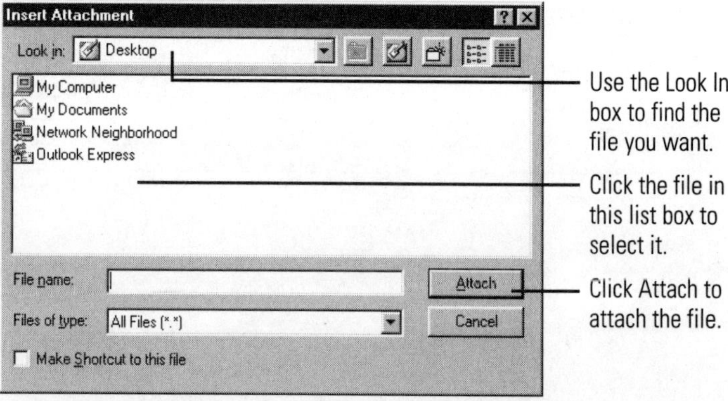

7. To post the article and its attachment, click the Send toolbar button. Outlook Express posts the article to the news server. (Again note, however, that it may take a while for the news server to make the message available.)

Some of you are curious, so I'll tell you

Okay, let's face up to a fact. One of the most notorious elements of the Internet is all the sexual material. Presumably, you already know this, right? You've read the articles about people being arrested. You've read the articles about pornography being stored on university and government computer **networks.** I'm not telling you stuff you don't already know, right? Since you already know all this stuff, you should know that a lot of the most controversial stuff is found in newsgroups. Now you know.

SEE ALSO Free Speech; PGP

NNTP

This acronym stands for Network News Transfer Protocol. You sometimes see NNTP used as an adjective to describe a news **server.** Other than this, though, you won't really have to use this acronym. You don't, for example, use the acronym NNTP in uniform resource locators (URLs).

SEE ALSO Newsgroup; Protocol

Offline Browsing

Internet Explorer and Outlook Express let you work offline. What this means, basically, is that you can browse web pages, work with e-mail, and do a bit of work with newsgroups even when you're not connected to the Internet. When you work offline, of course, you can't retrieve web pages from the Internet. So you work with web pages you've stored in your **document cache** on your hard disk or in your History folder, or web pages that you've set up for offline viewing.

If you want to work offline—by default Internet Explorer and Outlook Express assume you want to work online—choose the File menu's Work Offline command. (This command is available on the File menus of both Internet Explorer and Outlook Express.) If you try to retrieve a web page or some other item that hasn't been cached on your hard disk or you try to do something that requires a real connection, Internet Explorer or Outlook Express lets you know and asks if you want to make a connection.

continues

Offline Browsing *(continued)*

Internet Explorer lets you list web pages that you want to regularly view in an Offline Pages list. Once you set up a page for offline viewing, Internet Explorer will automatically check the web page to see if it's changed since the last time you viewed it and, if so, will download the web page so you can view it.

Making a Page Available Offline

To set up a web page for offline viewing, follow these steps:

1. Display the web page.
2. Choose the Favorites menu's Add To Favorites command. Internet Explorer displays the Add Favorite dialog box.

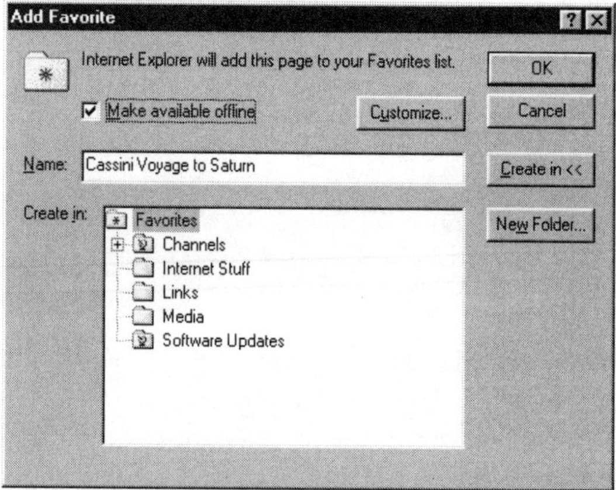

3. Select the Make Available Offline check box.
4. Click OK if you want your offline version of the page to be updated, or synchronized, only when you choose the Favorites menu's Synchronize command.
5. To set up a schedule or customize the way Internet Explorer synchronizes this page, click Customize to start the Offline Favorite Wizard.
6. The Offline Favorite Wizard will walk you through setting up a schedule to download the page; just follow the instructions.

Synchronizing Your Offline Pages

To synchronize the pages you set up for offline viewing, start Internet Explorer, choose the Tools menu's Synchronize command, and then click Synchronize.

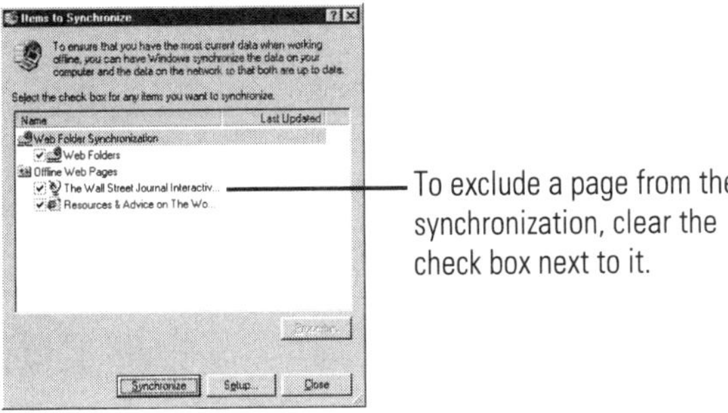

Changing a Page's Synchronization Schedule

To change when a page is synchronized for offline viewing, follow these steps:

1. Choose the Tools menu's Synchronize command.
2. Select the page you want to reschedule and then click Properties.
3. Click the Schedule tab.

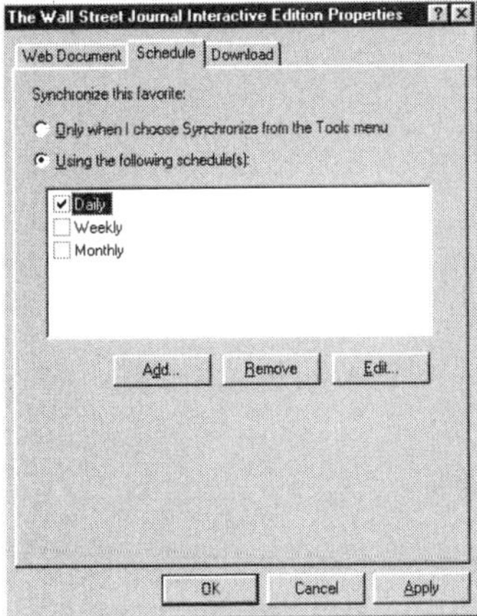

4. Click the Using The Following Schedule(s) option button, and then select a schedule from the list of schedules you've created.
5. To create a new schedule, click Add and describe the schedule in the New Schedule window.
6. If you connect to the Internet using a Dial-Up Networking connection and a modem, click Edit, and then click the Synchronization Items tab. Select the If My Computer Is Not Connected check box to tell Internet Explorer to automatically make an Internet connection to update your subscription.
7. Click OK when you're finished.

continues

Offline Browsing *(continued)*

Getting notification about newly synchronized pages

By default, Internet Explorer alerts you when subscription updates occur so that you can view updated web pages offline. You can change the way you receive this notification, however, by displaying the page's Properties dialog box, clicking the Download tab, and then using its buttons and boxes to specify how a subscription works.

Offline Pages SEE Offline Browsing

Online Services

The term *online services* refers to a big computer **network** with a bunch of good **files** and programs. Whoever owns this big computer network makes money by selling people like you and me access to the files stored on the network and by renting us programs on the network. Every online service, for example, provides **e-mail** so that you can e-mail other online service users. (Most online services—and perhaps all the online services—also provide e-mail **gateways** to the Internet.) Online services also provide you with other stuff. Usually, there are good games you can play, neat files you can download, and up-to-the-minute news services that let you know what's happening all over the world. **America Online** is an online service. So are CompuServe, Prodigy, and The **Microsoft** Network.

SEE ALSO **Downloading Files**

Outlook Express

Outlook Express is the e-mail **client** that comes with Internet Explorer, so this book assumes you'll use Outlook Express for **e-mail** and for **mailing lists.** You also use Outlook Express for working with **newsgroups.**

SEE ALSO **Quick Reference: Outlook Express Commands *and* Outlook Express Toolbar Guide**

Packets

Everything—all the information—that gets passed around the Internet is passed as a packet. When you send some piece of information, for example, it is broken down into packets by the sending computer and then reassembled by the receiving computer. In fact, this packetizing and unpacketizing is what the **TCP/IP** protocol does.

Password

You know what a password is, right? It's the secret word or code that you give to a computer, along with your username, to prove your identity. The logic of a password, of course, is that only the real user knows the real password, so access to the computer can be restricted to the person who is supposed to use it. There are, however, three rules concerning passwords. One rule is that your password shouldn't be easy to guess. (Don't use your name, for example.) The second rule is that you shouldn't forget your password. The third rule is that you should never tell anyone your password.

PC

A PC, or personal computer, is a computer marketed toward an average consumer. To be a little more specific, people usually use the term *PC* to refer to computers sold with an Intel-compatible CPU chip. These computers typically use the Microsoft Windows operating system, although some PCs run IBM's OS/2 or versions of UNIX. Palmtop computers and some other types of computers aren't really PCs, but as they become more mainstream, people may begin to refer to these computers as PCs too.

PDF SEE Acrobat Reader

PGP

PGP stands for Pretty Good Privacy; it is an encryption utility. It encrypts—or turns into coded messages—electronic files such as e-mail messages. Once a message has been encrypted using PGP, no one but the intended recipient can read it. So PGP is sort of interesting to people who use the Internet. Of more interest, however, is the story of how PGP was created and what happened to the creator.

Briefly, in the mid-1980s, a college student named Phillip Zimmerman read an article in the *Smithsonian* magazine that described encryption algorithms (calculation rules, basically) that made it nearly impossible for anyone other than the intended recipient to read messages. So what did the kid do? Shoot, he did what every good computer science student would do. Working on his own, he created a software program that implements the encryption algorithms.

Anyway, time goes by. By now it's the early 1990s and everything is cruising along smoothly—until one day when one of Zimmerman's friends posts Zimmerman's PGP utility on the Internet. The next thing you know, people around the world are downloading copies of this tool. And that was nice for them. But not for Zimmerman.

It turns out that the United States has strict export restrictions that severely limit the ability of Americans and American companies from selling or distributing encryption technology. And Zimmerman may have violated those export restrictions by making PGP available on the Internet, because the Internet is a global network. In fact, for a while the U.S. Attorney's office in San Jose was investigating Zimmerman's actions. He could have been imprisoned for as long as five years. And he could have been fined as much as $1 million. (At the time I'm writing this, things have apparently cooled off for Zimmerman.)

The story of PGP is a really good one, however, because it touches on a couple of important points about the Internet. First, the Internet is not a very secure network. Although not very likely, it's technically possible for text sent from one person to another over the Internet to be read by someone else not intended to read it.

(This is why, so the rumor mill says, the U.S. doesn't want encryption technology distributed abroad: the Central Intelligence Agency and the National Security Agency want to electronically eavesdrop on people.)

A second thing that the PGP story shows is that it's easier than you think to break the law. Maybe Zimmerman or his friend knew that distributing the implementation of the algorithm—the same algorithm described in an internationally distributed magazine—would violate an export restriction. But I'll bet you a cup of coffee they didn't know. Part of the culture of the Internet is that you give back, that you post valuable information or utilities for the benefit of other people. Yet by posting PGP, Zimmerman got into serious trouble.

And there are lots of other similar cases—situations in which an Internet user got into trouble by posting stuff. Right now, for example, two Californians are serving jail time for posting explicit pictures to adult **newsgroups.** Their pictures violated pornography laws in Tennessee, even though they posted the stuff in California and even though their material may not have violated pornography laws in California. And more than a few people have gotten into trouble by posting e-mail messages and newsgroup **articles** that made libelous statements about other people or companies.

So another lesson of the PGP story is that before you post anything anywhere, think carefully. You don't want to post something that violates a federal law or some obscure federal regulation. And you need to be careful, too, that you don't unwittingly break a local law in some other part of the country.

In a nutshell, how PGP works

How PGP works is sort of interesting. The whole encryption system relies on two keys, a public key and a private key. What you do (if you have PGP) is freely distribute the public key. Anyone who has PGP and your public key can use the public key to lock messages they send to you. Whenever you get a PGP-encrypted message, you unlock the message with the private key. The whole system works because, while anyone with the public key can lock a message, only the person with the correct private key can unlock it.

SEE ALSO Digital ID

Pine

Pine is a popular **e-mail** software program developed, coincidentally, by my alma mater, the University of Washington. If you're connecting to the Internet using a shell account and the HyperTerminal application, for example, there's a good chance you're using Pine. Because this book assumes that you're connecting to the Internet using Internet Explorer (which means you aren't using a **shell account**), I'm not going to provide any step-by-step instructions here.

Pirates SEE Hackers

PKZIP

PKZIP is a popular compression utility that scrunches files so they take up less space. How compression utilities scrunch files is beyond the scope of our little discussion. But if you frequently e-mail large attachments to people, you'll want to acquire and then regularly use a compression utility such as PKZIP. The reason is that scrunching a file makes it easier to move the file around the Internet. That makes sense, right? A file that is 100KB in size, all other factors being equal, will take longer to **download** and **upload** than a file that is 20KB in size.

You should be able to find an evaluation of PKZIP or **WinZip,** which is an equivalent compression utility at the following web site: *http://www.zdnet.com/*.

The dirt on compression

The amount of compression you get with PKZIP (and any other file compression utility, for that matter) varies wildly because it depends on the type of file you're compressing. Sometimes PKZIP doesn't reduce the size of a file very much at all. If you try to PKZIP a **GIF** file, for example, you'll often get no real compression. The same is true of a **JPEG** file. Other graphics file formats, however, scrunch to 1 or 2 percent of their original size. While compression can sometimes make files much, much smaller—and it's probably something you should try—it doesn't always deliver a benefit.

SEE ALSO Downloading Files

Plug-In

Web browsers like Internet Explorer use special programs, called plug-ins, to do work they're not capable of doing themselves. For example, Internet Explorer can't show audio clips, so to play these sorts of sounds, it uses an audio plug-in. Internet Explorer also can't run video clips, so to play videos, it uses a video plug-in. Web page animation often requires a plug-in, too.

Post SEE Newsgroup

PPP

PPP stands for Point-to-Point Protocol. It describes a method of connecting to the Internet in which your PC, for the duration of the connection, becomes a **host computer** on the Internet. The advantage of a PPP connection is that it simplifies the business of **downloading** and **uploading** files, as compared to just having a **shell account.** With a PPP connection, you can move **files** directly between another host and your PC. (If you use a shell account, you first move a file from some other host to your **Internet service provider's** computer and then from your Internet service provider's computer to your PC.) A PPP connection also lets you use a web **browser** such as Internet Explorer to browse the **World Wide Web.** The only disadvantages of a PPP connection are that Internet service providers usually charge more money for them and they are slightly more difficult to set up. (You either use the **Connection Wizard** or **Dial-Up Networking** to make a PPP connection.)

SEE ALSO Downloading Files; SLIP

Protocol

In the world of diplomacy, a "protocol" refers to the rules of etiquette and ceremony that diplomats and heads of state follow.

In the world of computers, "protocol" refers to the rules that two computers use to communicate. For example, "Don't send me data faster than I can receive it" is a very basic computer protocol.

SEE ALSO IP; TCP/IP

RealPlayer

RealPlayer is a **plug-in** that lets you play RealAudio audio and RealVideo video clips you retrieve from the Internet. Typically, you play RealAudio and RealVideo clips by clicking a **hyperlink** that points to the clip. When you click the hyperlink, Internet Explorer starts the RealPlayer plug-in.

Remote Access Service

Remote Access Service, another name for Dial-Up Networking, is the Windows feature that lets you connect your personal computer to the Internet. As a practical matter, you don't ever have much to do with Remote Access Service, or Dial-Up Networking, because the Connection Wizard sets up all the Remote Access Service stuff for you.

Resource

When I first started reading about the Internet, I kept stumbling across the term *resource.* I found it really confusing. It finally dawned on me that people used the term to refer to a bunch of different things that were all sort of alike.

People sometimes use the term as a catchall category to refer to an Internet service such as a **newsgroup**, the **World Wide Web,** or **FTP.** Other times, the word refers to specific servers—mail servers, news servers, World Wide Web servers, Gopher servers, FTP servers, and so on. Still other times it refers to specific files (and their locations).

I think the most accurate way to use the term is to refer to something that can be described with a uniform resource locator, or **URL.** That's the way I use the term in this book. I use it to refer both to servers and to specific files. This is probably all crystal clear to you now. And you're wondering why I had trouble in the first place.

ROT13

ROT13 is a code. People sometimes use it to encrypt **newsgroup** articles that they don't want other people to read by mistake. For example, if you posted an article with information or commentary that was offensive to some people, you could encrypt the article using the ROT13 code. By doing this, you'd be in effect warning people, "Hey, there's some pretty strong stuff in this message. You probably don't want to read it if you're easily offended."

The ROT13 code is easy to break, however. Anyone who really wants to can break the code and read a message that has been encrypted with the ROT13 code. In fact, Outlook Express's Edit menu includes a command, Unscramble (ROT13), that you can use to decrypt the newsgroup article shown in the message window. (This command only appears on the Edit menu when you've opened a newsgroup article in a message window.)

SEE ALSO Digital ID; Encryption

RTFM

You see this acronym in postings to **newbies** a lot. But I wouldn't suggest using it unless you know what the letter "F" stands for. The R, T, and M stand for "Read The Manual."

Scripting

Some communications applications provide a scripting feature. In a nutshell, a scripting feature types stuff for you such as your **username**, your **password**, and anything else you're supposed to type as you make a connection. To write a **Dial-Up Networking** script—let's say you aren't using the **Connection Wizard** but are instead doing things manually—you use the Dial-Up Scripting Tool.

Search Engine

Search engines are services that help you find what you're looking for on the Internet. These services are so valuable that most web **browsers** have a search tool or command that you can click to display a list of search engines.

continues

Search Engine *(continued)*

One other comment. Each search engine works a little differently, so you'll have to experiment to find which one best suits your needs. You'll also want to learn to use one search service really well. (You can do this by reading all the instructions provided by the search engine. You may have to follow a hyperlink titled Advanced Search or Search Options.)

Using a Search Engine

To use a search engine, click the Search toolbar button to display the Search Explorer bar. Choose a type of search and then enter the word or phrase you want the search engine to use in its search in the text box provided. (To narrow your search, be very specific.) When you click the search engine form's Start Search button (this might be named Start, Submit, Go, or something similar), the search engine looks through its index for web pages that use the word or phrase you entered. If the search engine finds web pages that use your word or phrase, it displays a results web page, which describes and provides **hyperlinks** to the web pages.

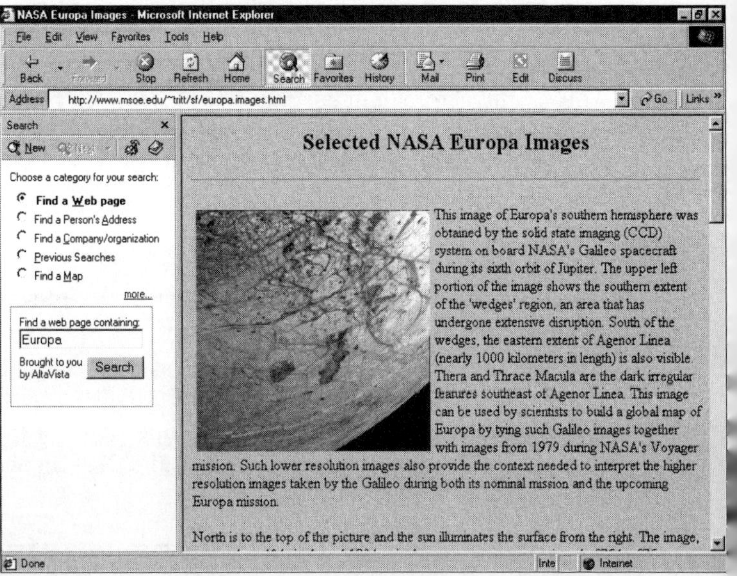

Using the Find command to search from the Address bar

To quickly perform a search using your default search engine, just type *find* followed by the word or phrase you would like to search for in the Address box.

Selecting a Search Engine

To select a search engine to use, follow these steps:

1. Click the Search toolbar button to display the Search Explorer bar.
2. Click Customize at the top of the Search Explorer bar.
3. Use the Customize Search Settings page to specify which search engines you want to use for each type of search.
4. Click Update or Reset to start over with your customizations.

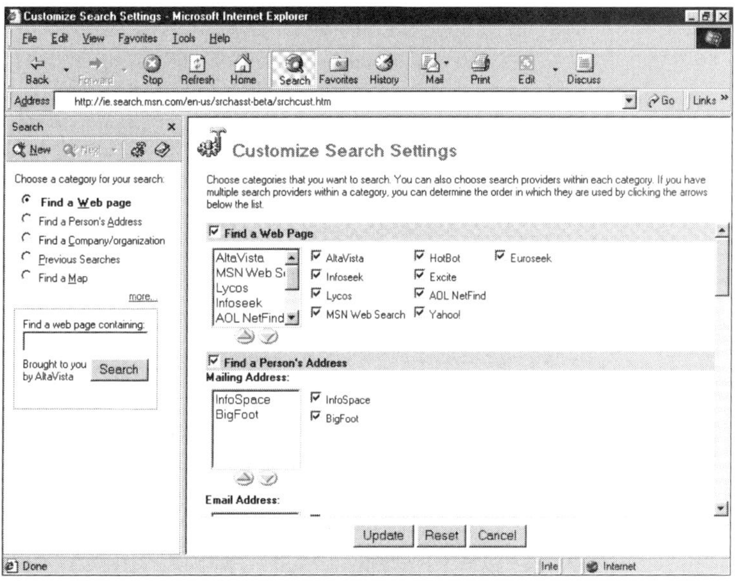

Secure Web Sites

Secure web sites are sites that use an **encryption** algorithm to ensure that **hackers** won't be able to intercept information, such as passwords or credit card numbers, that you send to the web site you're viewing. You have two ways of knowing whether you are viewing a secure web page. First, if the page is secured, you will see a small yellow lock on the Internet Explorer status bar at the bottom of the screen. Second, if the web page's address begins with https://, the *s* stands for *secure* http. Never make any purchases over the Internet with a credit card unless you are at a secure web site.

continues

Secure Web Sites *(continued)*

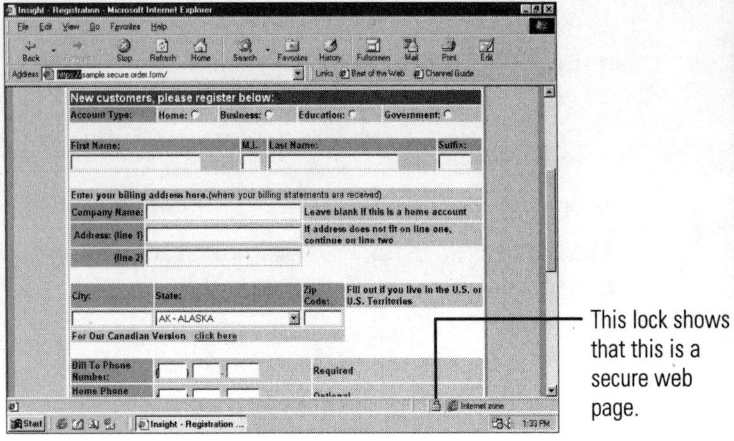

This lock shows that this is a secure web page.

Security Zones

Security Zones are a neat way of dividing up a big ocean into smaller ponds. Using Security Zones, for example, you can specify that you want to set your security level pretty low on your corporate **intranet**, while keeping it at a medium level for most of the Internet and at a very high level for some selected sites that you don't feel so sure about.

Setting Up Security Zones

To change your Security Zones, choose the View menu's Internet Options command. Click the Security tab. In the Zone list box, select the zone you want to edit, and then move the slider to set a security level for that zone.

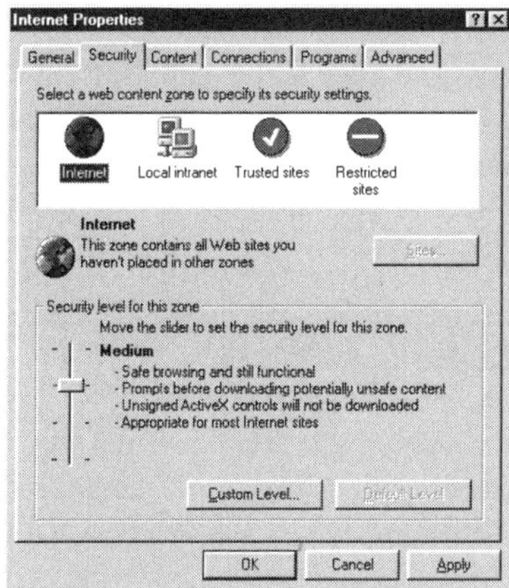

To add sites to the Trusted Sites zone or to the Restricted Access zone, select the zone from the Zone list box and then click Add Sites. Type the **URL** for the site in the text box, and then click Add.

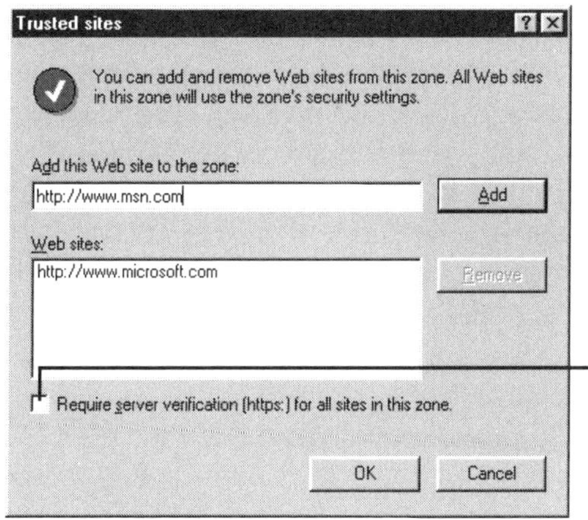

Select this check box to specify that only secure web sites can be in the Trusted Sites zone.

Server

When you use your **PC** to connect directly to another **host computer**—for example, when you use a **Dial-Up Networking** connection—your PC is called a **client.** The other host computer is a server. Since we're on the topic, I may as well also say that the software that runs on the client is client software. And the software that runs on the server is—big surprise here—server software.

continues

Server *(continued)*

One point that's good to remember is that to do just about anything, your client software and the server software need to work together. Oftentimes you can't accomplish some task, even though the client and its software work, because either the server or its software doesn't work.

Server Extensions

Server extensions are small programs that run on a web **server**. There are two types of server extensions worth knowing about: FrontPage server extensions and Office server extensions.

FrontPage server extensions allow users to easily save web pages to a web server if they have the Microsoft FrontPage or Microsoft Office 2000 programs. They also allow the easy creation of small web page programs, such as counters.

Office server extensions are meant for businesses, supporting everything FrontPage server extensions can, as well as group-based features such as interactive group discussions embedded in a document. You can also use Office server extensions to subscribe to a particular document on the Web. Then when someone other than you changes the document, you receive an e-mail message telling you that the document was changed. In order to use Office server extensions, you need Office 2000.

Sex

There's a ton of sexually oriented material in Internet **newsgroups.** There are also a huge number of World Wide Web sites that offer sexual material. Some of this stuff is tame, and some is very explicit. Some of this stuff qualifies as art. And some of it is disgusting. I think the disgusting stuff mostly appears in newsgroups without moderators. But I'm not sure. I have not done exhaustive research on this.

If you don't want your kids (or anyone else) accessing sexually oriented sites on the Internet, you have a few options. Several programs, such as Cyber Patrol and Cybersitter, do an increasingly good job of stopping the smut. You might also want to use a **search engine** to look for Internet filtering and blocking programs, or check *www.zdnet.com* for a recent review of such programs. However, no matter how good a program you buy, the bottom line is that these programs are only supplemental in nature. There is no substitute for being involved with a young person's Internet usage.

SEE ALSO Free Speech

Shareware

Shareware is software that you can **download** for free. If you like the software or intend to use it, you are supposed to send a small fee to the programmer who created it. Some shareware applications have code written into them that makes the programs inoperable unless users pay the fee within a certain period of time. In addition to computer applications, clip art collections and font files are distributed as shareware. In fact, I think it's fair to say that the Internet's **FTP** sites and **newsgroups** are chock-full of shareware.

Freeware, a variation of shareware, is given away absolutely free. You don't have to send any money to the programmer who invented it, although most programmers ask for a postcard or some other gratis acknowledgment. I guess they want to know who's using their software.

Shell Account

With a shell account, you use a communications application like HyperTerminal to connect to an **Internet service provider.** Your PC becomes, in effect, just a monitor and keyboard attached to the Internet service provider's **host computer.** Although shell accounts were once commonplace among Internet users, most people now use **Dial-Up Networking** accounts because they are easier to use and they allow users to graphically browse the World Wide Web.

SEE ALSO Connections; Telnet

Shortcut Icons

Windows lets you place icons for commonly used documents, web pages, programs, folders, and other stuff like this on the desktop. This maybe doesn't seem like all that neat of a deal, but it is. By putting one of these icons, called shortcut icons, on the desktop, you can open a program such as Internet Explorer or some other Internet client with a simple double-click. (The Internet setup program adds a shortcut icon for Internet Explorer and Outlook Express to the desktop.

Shouting

If you type an e-mail message or a newsgroup article in all capital letters, it's called shouting. BUT YOU SHOULDN'T DO THIS. IT'S ANNOYING AS ALL GET OUT. What's more, type in all capital letters is hard to read.

SEE ALSO **Netiquette**

Signature

A signature is just an extra little bit of text you attach to the end of every e-mail message you send. If you use Outlook Express as your e-mail program, you can add signatures to your e-mail messages.

Adding a Signature with Outlook Express

To add a signature to your e-mail messages, follow these steps:

1. Start Outlook Express.
2. Choose the Tools menu's Options command.
3. Click the Signatures tab.

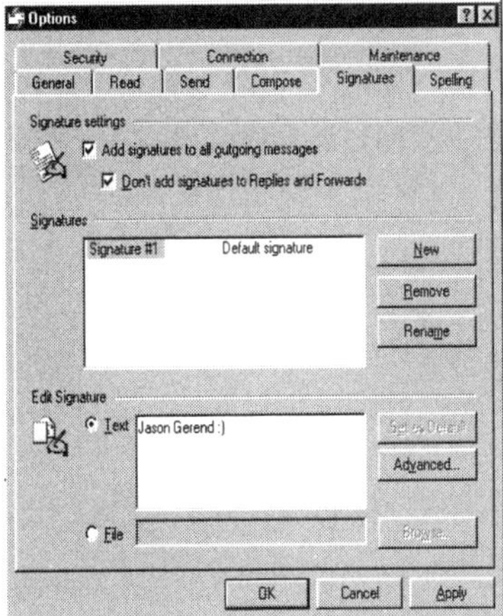

4 Click New to create a new signature.

5 Enter the text you want in the Signature Settings text box.

6 If you already have a text or HTML signature file, click the File option button and then click Browse to locate your file. Select the file, click Open, and then click OK.

7 Select the Add Signatures To All Outgoing Messages check box, and click OK.

SLIP

SLIP is an acronym for Serial Line Internet Protocol. Like **PPP,** it is a method of directly connecting to the Internet. When you make a SLIP connection, your PC becomes a **host computer** on the Internet for the duration of the connection. The advantage of a SLIP connection (and a PPP connection) is that it simplifies the business of **downloading** and **uploading** files, as compared to a **shell account** connection. With a SLIP or PPP connection, you move a file only once (from the host that acts as the **server** to your PC) rather than twice (first from the host that acts as the server to the **Internet service provider's** computer and then from the Internet service provider's computer to your PC).

A SLIP connection also lets you do things like browse the World Wide Web. The only two disadvantages of a SLIP connection are that Internet service providers usually charge more money for them and they are slightly more difficult to set up. (You use the **Dial-Up Networking** program to make a SLIP connection.)

continues

Slip *(continued)*

SLIP vs. PPP

If you have a choice between a PPP or SLIP connection, choose PPP. PPP is pretty much the standard these days. Plus, PPP is faster than SLIP. What's more, it's easier to set up a PPP connection. No matter how you got Windows on your machine, you have all the stuff you need already. (The SLIP stuff comes only on the CD version of Windows.) Finally, some of the work you have to do to set up a SLIP connection is rather complicated. You have to worry about IP header compression, for example. Yuck.

Smileys

E-mail, like any writing, isn't a very precise communication tool. It's easy to say too much, too little, or to leave the reader confused or angry. And this is true even if you're the world's greatest living novelist (or so I imagine). To deal with the limitations of the written word in e-mail, people sometimes add smileys, also called emoticons, to their messages. In essence, a smiley is a face you make with symbol keys. For example, by combining the colon with the end parenthesis mark—turn the page sideways to see this—you get a smiley face. Sort of. :) And if you combine the colon with the begin parenthesis mark, you get a frowning face. : (Lots of people—and you may be one—find it helpful to use these faces to say what their prose doesn't say. Do smileys work? I don't know. You be the judge:

> Sue,
>
> I'm sorry I missed you.
>
> I thought we had a date. But I guess not.
>
> See you around the playground.
>
> Steve
>
> : (

Snail Mail

Snail mail is what Internet users sometimes call the regular mail. You know, the kind with letters, envelopes, stamps, and letter carriers. Whereas it may take days, weeks, or even months for an airmail letter to reach some parts of the world, an e-mail message can move around the world in a matter of seconds. (I should probably tell you, however, that **e-mail** isn't always this fast, nor is it 100 percent reliable. Sometimes an e-mail message can take hours, days, or even weeks to reach its destination if the mail **servers** that do the work of delivering the message are slow or shut down.)

Spam

Spam refers to junk **e-mail.** Although spam may sound innocuous at first blush, it actually represents a big problem. Let me explain. What happens with spam is that somebody who wants to sell something—lets say it's investment advice—builds a list of thousands and thousands of **e-mail addresses.** (Special spam mailing programs can do this by looking at the e-mail names and addresses of the people who post messages to **newsgroups** and by looking at online directories of e-mail names and addresses.) Once the spammer has this list, he begins sending huge volleys of junk e-mail messages to the names on his mailing list. He may also sell his mailing list to other spammers. Suddenly you have thousands and thousands of spammers all sending thousands and thousands of junk e-mail messages. This affects you personally in at least two ways: First, you may rather quickly find your Inbox littered with junk e-mail messages (which causes all the same problems that junk **snail mail** does). Second, the high volume of spam that's being passed around the Internet—on some mail servers spam accounts for 80 to 90 percent of the message volume—means that spam wastes **bandwidth.**

SEE ALSO Flame; Netiquette

Start Page

A start page is the first **World Wide Web** document you view with a web **browser** such as **Internet Explorer.** (Sometimes people also call start pages by another name, **home pages.**) You can tell your web browser which start page, or home page, it should display when you first start it. Or you can just use whatever start page the web browser is initially set to use.

Changing Your Start Page

You can specify which web page you want Internet Explorer to display when you start the program and when you click the Home toolbar button. The easiest way to do this is to first display the web page you want to use as your start page. Next, choose the View menu's Internet Options command. In the Internet Options dialog box, click the General tab, and then click Use Current.

Returning to Your Start Page

To return to your start page, click the Home toolbar button.

Stationery

Outlook Express, the e-mail client that comes with Internet Explorer, lets you use nicely formatted, professionally designed templates as the basis of the **e-mail** messages you create. With these templates—Outlook Express calls them stationery—you don't have to do any special formatting to your message. All you do is add the text.

To create a new e-mail message that uses stationery, start Outlook Express and then click the down arrow next to the New Mail toolbar button. Outlook Express displays a submenu that lists the stationery choices you have. Select the command that corresponds to the stationery you want to use. Then compose your e-mail message in the usual way.

Keep in mind that if the person you're e-mailing doesn't have an e-mail program capable of receiving messages in HTML format, they will see only plain text. I usually send a message with stationery to someone and then ask them if they saw a cool font and picture. If they say no, I don't send any more messages with stationery to them.

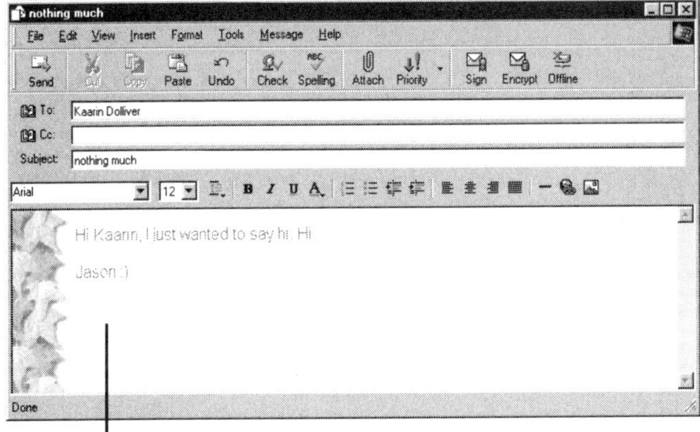

This is the Ivy stationery.

Status Bar

The status bar is the bar that runs across the bottom of the window in Internet Explorer, Outlook Express, and just about every other Windows program. The status bar tells you the current status of the program or your latest operation. To turn on the status bar in Internet Explorer, choose the View menu's Status Bar command. In Outlook Express, choose the View menu's Layout command. In the Window Layout Properties dialog box, select the Status Bar check box.

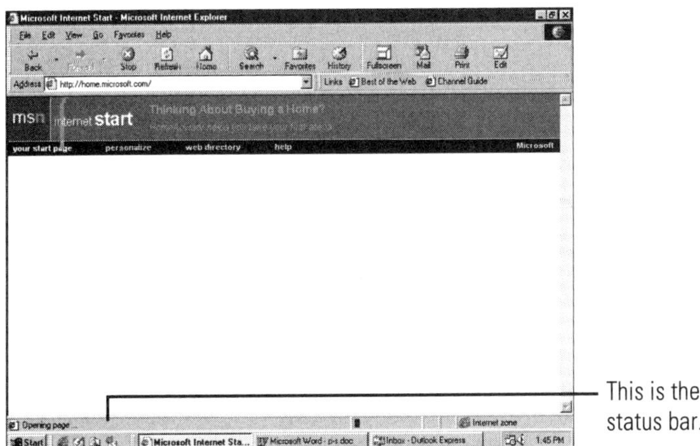

This is the status bar.

Style Sheets SEE CSS

Subfolder

This book uses the term *subfolder* to refer to a folder within a folder. Some people might also call a subfolder a subdirectory.

Subscriptions SEE Offline Browsing

Switching Tasks

To switch tasks in Windows, use the Taskbar. The Taskbar is the bar along the bottom of the screen. (If Internet Explorer is set to full screen, click the Fullscreen toolbar button to display the Taskbar.) The Taskbar shows the Start button on the left side. To the right of the Start button are buttons that represent applications that are open.

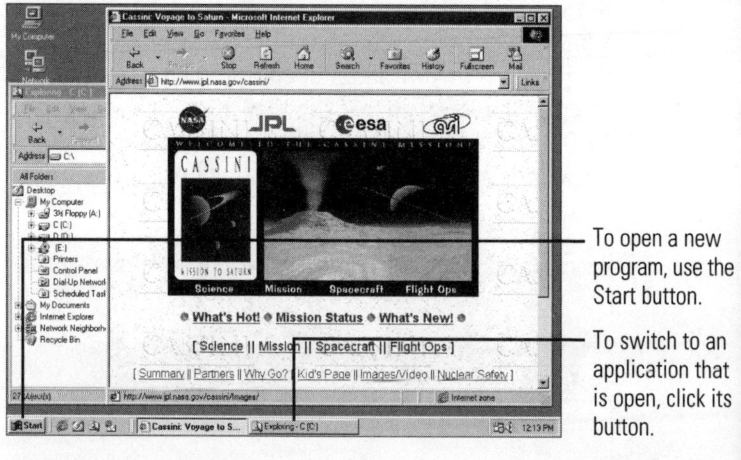

SEE ALSO Multitasking

T1 Transmission Line

A T1 transmission line connects **host computers** and passes information at a rate of 1.5Mbps. That's pretty fast. The table that follows lists the download speeds for several modems and transmission lines:

Modem or line	Transmission speed (download)
2400bps modem	2,400 bits (1s or 0s) per second
28.8K modem	28,800 bits per second
56K modem	53,000 bits per second
ISDN line	64,000 or 128,000 bits per second
ADSL line	256,000 bits per second to 8,000,000 bits per second
Cable modem	Up to 30,000,000 bits per second
1.5Mbps T1 line	1,500,000 bits per second
T3 line	45,000,000 bits per second

When I first heard about T1 transmission lines, I thought I needed one. Partly for the **bandwidth,** but also because my brother has one (he does research at a university). Alas, I soon learned that T1 lines are very, very expensive. Even if you have a short connection to make to another nearby **host computer,** you'll pay at least several hundred dollars a month—and very possibly a couple of thousand dollars a month. If you have a long connection to make to a faraway host computer, you could pay thousands of dollars a month. So I don't have a T1 transmission line.

High bandwidth doesn't always equal high performance

Many otherwise sophisticated people share a common misconception concerning those high-bandwidth transmission lines I just mentioned. Even if you do have a T1 line pumping data into your computer at 1.5Mbps, many web sites won't feed you data that fast. The burden of hundreds or thousands of simultaneous users can quickly bring the fastest web server to its knees, leaving you twiddling your thumbs at the same rate as someone with a 28.8Kbps modem.

SEE ALSO Baud; Cable Modem

T3 Transmission Line

A T3 transmission line moves data at a rate of 45Mbps. That's really fast. In fact, the old NSFnet **backbone** used T3 transmission lines. And **online services** such as The **Microsoft Network** use T3 transmission lines as well.

SEE ALSO T1 Transmission Line

TCP/IP

TCP/IP is the **protocol** that describes how information gets passed around the Internet. (A protocol is essentially a set of rules.) TCP/IP breaks information into **packets,** routes those packets from the sending computer to the receiving computer, and finally reassembles the packets after they reach the receiving computer. If a packet is missing—say it gets lost somewhere on its trip from the sending computer—TCP/IP directs the sending computer to send another copy of the missing packet.

TCP/IP stands for Transmission Control Protocol/Internet Protocol, if you care to know, and I wouldn't blame you if you didn't.

Telnet

When you telnet, you **log on** to another computer or **network.** Okay. This sounds kooky, I know. But say you're logged on to an **Internet service provider's** computer or network. And you've been noodling around. Using a telnet command, you can probably log on to another computer network. In other words, even if you are 5000 miles away from the computer or network you want to log on to, you can use the Internet to make the connection.

Windows comes with a telnet client. To use it, you can enter the uniform resource locator (**URL**) for a telnet site in the Internet Explorer Address box, you can click on a **hyperlink** that points to a telnet site, or you can start the telnet client directly using **Windows Explorer.**

Starting a Telnet Session with Internet Explorer

As mentioned in the preceding paragraph, you can start a telnet session with Internet Explorer in two ways: you can enter the URL for the telnet site in the Address box, and you can click a hyperlink that points to a telnet site.

To enter the URL for a telnet site in the Address box, click the Address box to select its contents and then type the URL. Note that telnet sites start with the prefix "telnet://." When you press the Enter key, Internet Explorer starts the telnet client and instructs it to connect to the telnet site you identified.

To connect to a telnet site by clicking a hyperlink, just click the hyperlink. (The hyperlink provides the telnet site's URL.) Internet Explorer starts the telnet client, and it connects to the telnet site identified with the hyperlink.

After you connect to the telnet site, follow the on-screen instructions provided by the telnet site.

Starting a Telnet Session with the Telnet Client

To start a telnet session without Internet Explorer, first start the telnet client by choosing the Start menu's Run command and typing *telnet*. Then to make your telnet connection, follow these steps:

1. Choose the Connect menu's Remote System command. (If you haven't yet connected to your Internet service provider, this is when Windows makes the PPP connection.)

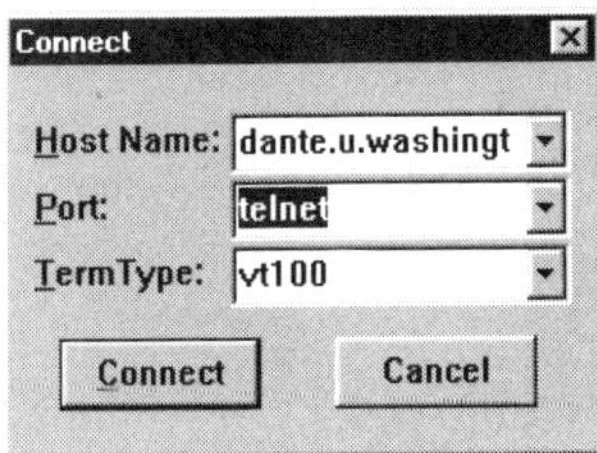

2. If necessary, enter the telnet **port** number in the Port drop-down list box.
3. If necessary, specify a terminal emulation type by using the TermType drop-down list box.
4. Click Connect. Telnet makes the connection. Next you see either the logon screen for the telnet site (it asks for a username or user ID and a password) or the main menu if there isn't a formal logon.

Ending a Telnet Session

To end a telnet session, choose the Connect menu's Disconnect command. To stop the Telnet program and close the Telnet window, click the Telnet window's Close box.

SEE ALSO Troubleshooting: Telnet

Temporary Internet Files SEE Document Cache

SEE Document Cache

Thread

As you might know, the messages that people post to **newsgroups** are called **articles.** You might also know that people can post articles that respond to other articles. The original article that someone posts along with any responses that other people post is called a thread.

Toolbars

Toolbars are rows of icons used to quickly perform common tasks. They're displayed near the top of a window in most Windows programs.

Customizing the Toolbar Area in Internet Explorer

To customize the toolbar area in Internet Explorer, simply right-click it, select which toolbars you would like to show, and optionally choose the Customize command to customize the buttons.

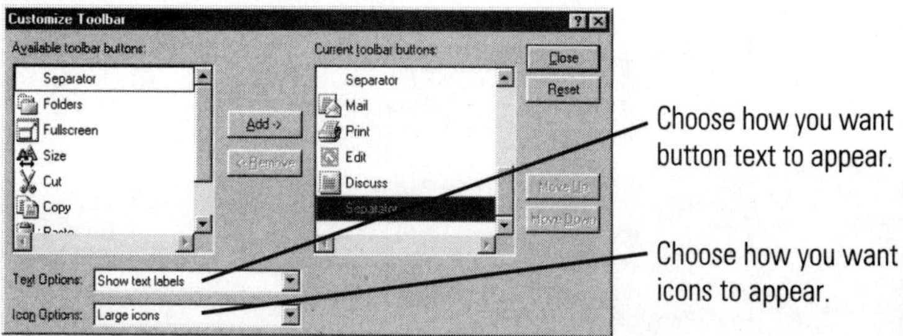

Outlook Express's toolbar

Customizing the toolbar in Outlook Express is really easy; right-click the toolbar, choose the Buttons command, and then rearrange those buttons to your heart's content.

Uniform Resource Locator SEE URL

UNIX

If you're going to surf the Internet, you may come into frequent contact with UNIX because many Internet **hosts** use UNIX. (This might happen, for example, if you **telnet** to a UNIX host.) Since this is a book on using Internet Explorer for Windows, I'm not going to get into the nitty gritty of UNIX commands or operating systems—I'd just be wasting your time.

Uploading Files

Uploading files is what you do when you copy a file from your computer to a **host** computer, or **server,** on the Internet. To upload a file, you can either use Internet Explorer's built-in **FTP** functions or **Web Publishing Wizard.** If you have a Microsoft Office 2000 product and an **Internet service provider** supporting Office or Microsoft FrontPage **server extensions,** you can use the program's Save To The Web feature to upload files as easily as saving to your hard drive.

SEE ALSO **Downloading Files**

URL

The uniform resource locator, or URL, specifies how you find an Internet **resource.** There are four parts to a URL: the service or **protocol;** the **server** name; the path; and the document, or file, name.

A Sample URL Explained

Let me explain each part of a URL by using a real-life Web page—the one that provides biographical data on the President of the United States and his family.

`http://www.whitehouse.gov/EOP/OP/html/OP_Bio.html.`

http:// identifies this resource as part of the **World Wide Web.**

www.whitehouse.gov/ identifies the server. (Notice that *whitehouse.gov* is really a **domain name.**)

WH/glimpse/presidents/html/ names the directory and subdirectory within the World Wide Web document.

bc42.html names the World Wide Web document.

continues

URL *(continued)*

Reviewing the Other Services and Protocols

The World Wide Web is only one of the services available on the Internet. Not surprisingly then, URLs use other codes to identify the other services and protocols. Here's a list of codes with some examples and additional comments:

Service *or* protocol	Explanation
file://	Refers to a file on the local computer.
ftp://	Refers to the file transfer protocol.
http://	Refers to the HyperText Transfer Protocol **(HTTP)**, which is what you use to browse the World Wide Web.
news://	Refers to the network news transfer protocol, which is what you use to browse **newsgroups**.
telnet://	Used to start a **telnet** session.

The URL blues

You can make a couple of easy mistakes when it comes to URLs. One is to mistakenly use backward slashes (\) instead of forward slashes (/). For example, the correct URL is *http://www.microsoft.com/*, not *http:\\www.microsoft.com*. The other easy mistake concerns case. **UNIX** operating systems recognize case (lower vs. upper) in filenames, although not in server names. So if the URL is *http://www.blah.com/file.html* and you enter *http://www.blah.com/FILE.HTML*, it probably won't work. Note, however, that the URLs *http://www.blah.com/file.html* and *http://WWW.BLAH.COM/file.html* are equivalent. In other words, case doesn't matter for the server name. Let me say one last thing. You'll usually be fine if you use all lowercase letters.

SEE ALSO HTML

Usenet Newsgroups SEE Newsgroup

Username

When you **log on** to a **network**, the network wants to know your identity. To identify yourself, give your name or username. Your username is also typically the first part of your Internet **e-mail address**.

SEE ALSO Authentication; Internet Explorer

Uuencode

As a general rule, e-mail messages and **newsgroup articles** must be composed entirely of text. This means that you can't include binary files in an e-mail message or newsgroup article. You can't e-mail someone a program file because program files aren't text files, for example. And you can't post a picture to a newsgroup because graphics image files aren't text files.

To deal with this limitation, early Internet users created a program called uuencode. Uuencode converts binary files to text files so they can be included in e-mail messages and posted as newsgroup articles. (This is called uuencoding.) It also converts these text files back into binary files. (Some people call this uudecoding.) With uuencode, therefore, you or your computer goes to an extra bit of work to send or receive binary files. But you can do it.

People still use uuencode. You'll see many uuencoded files in Internet newsgroups, for example. But with **Outlook Express** (which is what you'll want to use for **e-mail** and for newsgroup browsing), you don't need to worry about uuencoding or uudecoding binary files. Outlook Express automatically does this for you.

SEE ALSO MIME

Viewer

To look at a graphics file, such as a **GIF** or **JPEG** file, or to look at a movie file, such as a **MPEG** file or **AVI** file, you need a viewer. A viewer is just a program that opens graphics files and movie files. Windows comes with a viewer that lets you look at AVI files, the Media Player. Internet Explorer comes with an internal viewer that lets you look at GIF and JPEG files. To open an MPEG file, you need an MPEG viewer.

You can often find **shareware** and freeware viewers at the *http://www.zdnet.com/* web site.

SEE ALSO Encoded Files

Virus

A virus is a program created by a pathetic little wimp with a bit of technical knowledge but zero maturity, zero common sense, and zero morals. The virus program this loser creates often attempts to destroy either your computer or the data stored on your computer's hard disk.

You get viruses by using infected floppy disks or infected software on your computer. You also get viruses by **downloading** infected **files** from the Internet. This can include opening e-mail messages with attached files or embedded **ActiveX** programs. A good guideline is if you receive an e-mail message with an attachment from somebody you don't know, check the attached file for viruses before opening it.

If your machine does get a virus or if you're wondering whether your machine has one, you can probably locate and eradicate it by using an anti-virus program. You can usually get evaluation copies of anti-virus programs from the *http://www.mcafee.com/* and the *http://www.symantec.com/* web sites.

VRML

VRML stands for Virtual Reality Modeling Language and is the standard for Internet-based three-dimensional interactive worlds. To view VRML worlds, you need to have a VRML **viewer** installed. Internet Explorer comes with a VRML viewer that you can download or install from your CD-ROM.

VT100

Many years ago, Digital Equipment Corporation, a computer hardware manufacturer, created a terminal called the VT100. Because this terminal was so popular, it became a sort of de facto terminal standard. As a result, many terminals (and personal computers that emulate terminals) must pretend to be VT100s when they connect to **BBSs** (bulletin board systems) and **Internet service providers.** And, more important, the Windows's **telnet** client emulates a VT100 terminal when you use it for telnet sessions.

I mention this here because if you don't want the telnet client to emulate a VT100 terminal, you need to slightly change the way telnet works. To do this, start the telnet client (if necessary) and then choose the Terminal menu's Preferences command. When telnet displays the Preferences dialog box, use its boxes and buttons to tell telnet which type of terminal it should emulate.

W^3 SEE World Wide Web

Wallet

Microsoft Wallet lets you safely store your payment information on your computer so that it's easier to shop online. Wallet, then, saves you time because you enter this information only once. Or at least this is true if the online store where you shop knows about Wallet.

Installing Wallet

To install Wallet, click the Start button and then choose Settings and Control Panel. Double-click the Add/Remove Programs icon. Select Microsoft Internet Explorer from the list, and click Add/Remove. Select the Add A Component To Internet Explorer option button, and then click OK. Click OK when a dialog box asks you whether it is okay to determine what components are installed on your system. Scroll down until you find Microsoft Wallet, click to place a check mark next to it, and then click Next. Choose a download site, and then click Install Now.

Storing Credit Card Information with Wallet

To store credit card information with Wallet, follow these steps:

1. Start Internet Explorer if necessary.
2. Choose the View menu's Internet Options command. Internet Explorer displays the Options dialog box.
3. Click the Content tab.
4. Click Wallet. Internet Explorer displays the Payment Options dialog box.

continues

Wallet *(continued)*

(Internet Explorer may prompt you to install the credit card extensions; to do this, simply click Install.)

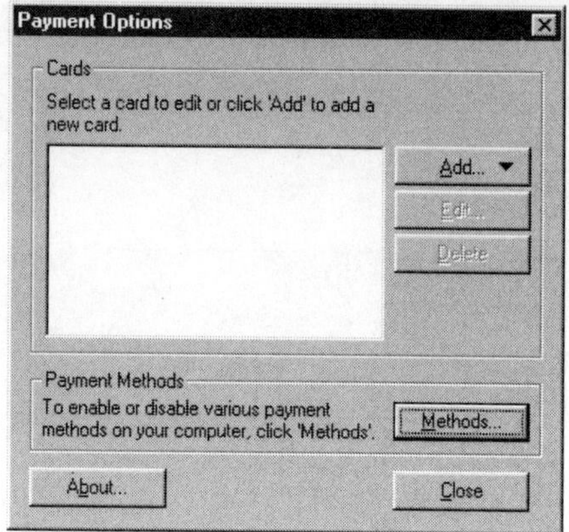

5 Click Add. Internet Explorer displays the Add menu. Then choose a credit card from the menu.

6 Wallet starts the Add A New Credit Card Wizard, which walks you through the steps of describing the credit card you want to use with Wallet.

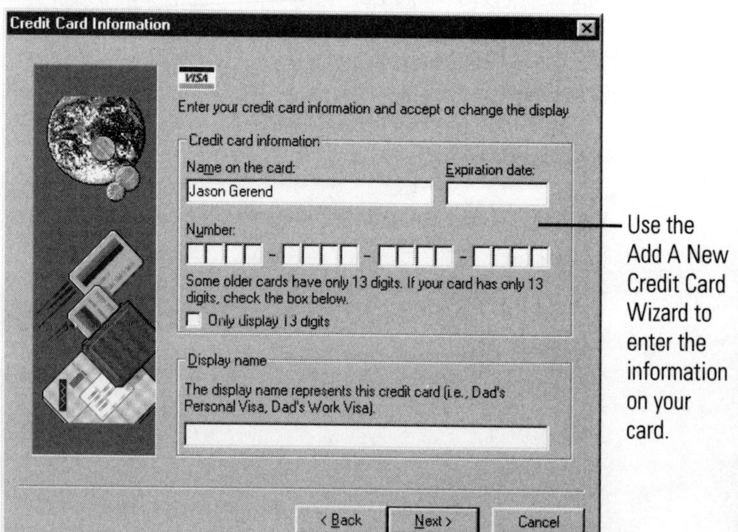

Use the Add A New Credit Card Wizard to enter the information on your card.

WAN

Do network acronyms ever stop? I guess not. WAN stands for wide area network, as in a **network** that includes computers across the state, province, shire, or country.

SEE ALSO LAN

Web SEE World Wide Web

Web Browsing

To browse the **World Wide Web,** you first make a **Dial-Up Networking** connection and then you use **Internet Explorer** to open and display World Wide Web documents.

Starting Internet Explorer

To start Internet Explorer, double-click the Internet Explorer icon, which appears on your **desktop.** If necessary, Internet Explorer makes a Dial-Up Networking connection. (You may need to provide information such as your **username** or **password** to make this connection.) After Internet Explorer makes the connection, it downloads and then displays your **start page.**

Note that if you're already connected to the Internet—say, because you're already using another Internet **client**—you won't need to make the connection again. So you won't see the dialog box that provides your username, password, and **Internet service provider's** telephone number.

Viewing the World Wide Web

After you've loaded your start page, you can view it by scrolling up and down. To move to another World Wide Web document, click a **hyperlink** in the currently displayed document. (The mouse pointer changes to a pointing finger whenever it rests over a hyperlink.) You can also move to another World Wide Web document by entering a new **URL** in the Address box. To move back and forth between World Wide Web pages you've already viewed, click the Back and Forward toolbar buttons.

Viewing Graphics with Internet Explorer

Internet Explorer comes with **GIF** and **JPEG** viewers built right into it. Sometimes you can click the image or its icon to move to a full-screen image. (You'll be able to tell when this is the case. The Internet Explorer status bar will say that the image is a shortcut to some other file.)

continues

Web Browsing *(continued)*

Why the image changes

If you look closely, you'll notice that some graphics images in World Wide Web documents look fuzzy at first but then become more and more focused. What you're seeing, just in case you care, is something called progressive rendering: as the World Wide Web server sends its image to your PC, your PC keeps drawing a better and clearer image the more information it gets.

Printing World Wide Web Documents

Internet Explorer's File menu provides a Print command. You can use it to print the web document shown in the Internet Explorer window. To use the File Print command, display the web page you want to print, choose the command, and then click OK when Internet Explorer displays the Print dialog box.

Saving World Wide Web Documents and Images

Internet Explorer's File menu provides a Save As command. You can use it to save the World Wide Web page you see on your screen. To use this command, just choose it. When Internet Explorer displays the Save Web Page dialog box, use the File Name box to name the document.

To save an image, right-click the image and then choose the shortcut menu's Save Picture As command. Then use the Save Picture dialog box to specify where to save the file.

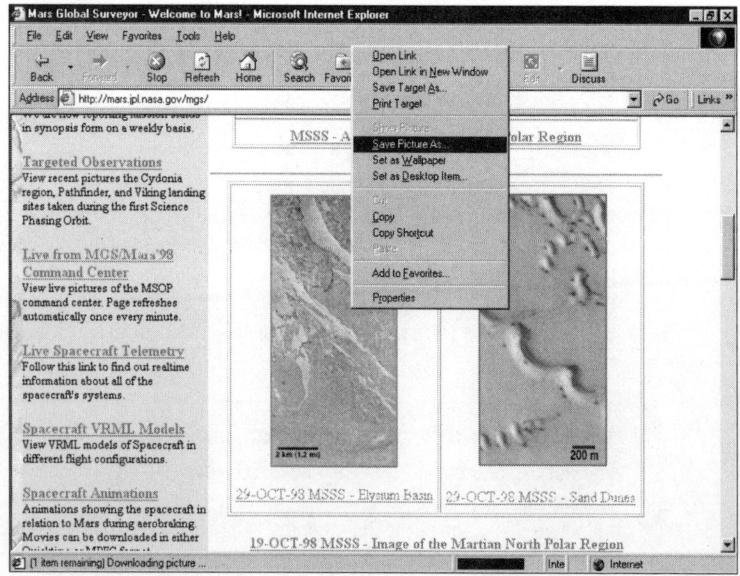

You can save full-screen GIF and JPEG images displayed in the Internet Explorer window by choosing the File menu's Save As command. Use the Save In and File Name boxes to specify where you want the file saved and what you want it named.

To view a GIF or JPEG file you've previously saved to disk using Internet Explorer, choose the File menu's Open command. When Internet Explorer displays the Open dialog box, click Browse. When Internet Explorer displays the Open dialog box, click the Files Of Type box down arrow, select either the GIF or JPEG file type, and then use the Look In and File Name boxes to locate and identify the file.

Disconnecting from the Internet

To disconnect your PC from the Internet, simply stop the Internet client programs you've started. Windows then asks if you want to disconnect from your Internet service provider. Indicate that you do by clicking Disconnect.

SEE ALSO **FTP; Internet Explorer; Quick Reference: Internet Explorer Commands *and* Internet Explorer Toolbar Guide; Telnet**

WebCrawler SEE Search Engine

Webmaster

A webmaster is just someone who creates **web pages** and then places, or publishes, these web pages on a web **server** so that other people can view them. If you're considering becoming a webmaster for your own site, by the way, you should know two essential pieces of information. First of all, the actual work of creating your own web pages and then publishing them isn't difficult. **Internet Explorer** even comes with a simple web-creation tool called Microsoft **FrontPage Express** and a handy web-publishing tool called **Web Publishing Wizard.** A second thing you should know is that the really hard work of publishing a web page is creating or locating the information you want to share.

SEE ALSO **Server Extensions**

Web Page

Web page is another name for the **HTML** document you view using a web **browser** like Internet Explorer. The World Wide Web, as you can guess, is made up of these web pages.

Web Publisher SEE Webmaster

Web Publishing Wizard

The Web Publishing Wizard lets you publish **HTML** documents, or web pages, to a web **server** that's part of an **intranet** or maintained by your **Internet service provider.** Once you've created your web pages (perhaps using Microsoft **FrontPage Express**), you start the wizard by clicking the Start button and then choosing Programs, Internet Explorer, and then Web Publishing Wizard. To use the wizard, just follow the on-screen instructions.

Web Site

Web site can refer to a couple of things. In this book, I use it to refer to a collection of web pages that a web publisher has created. Microsoft, for example, has a Microsoft Investor web site that provides a bunch of web pages with information of interest to investors. The United States Internal Revenue Service has a web site that provides information of interest to taxpayers.

Some people also use the term *web site* to refer to a web **server.** I don't think, however, that this is a good way to use the term. It makes more sense (to me at least) to just call a web server a web server.

White Pages

White-pages web sites are like electronic address books. You can use white pages to look up someone's **e-mail address** or even their real address and telephone number. One of the largest white pages is Bigfoot, which you can use and learn more about by visiting the web site at *http:/www.bigfoot.com/*. Several search engines have their own white and yellow pages. You can also use a search engine to search on the phrase "white pages" for a list of other white pages.

Wildcard Characters

Wildcard characters stand in for other characters in an expression. For example, you can use wildcard characters to stand in for characters in a **filename** when you're searching for a **file,** and you can use them as part of a command. The most common wildcard characters are the question mark (?) and asterisk (*) symbols. A question mark can stand for any single character. An asterisk can stand

for any single character, any group of characters, or for no group of characters at all. For example, if you wanted to search your hard drive for all of the JPEG images you have, you would search for *.jpg.

Windows Explorer

Windows Explorer lets you do things: It lets you view and work with your computer's disks and the **files** that are stored on your disk. It also lets you view and work with the other parts of your computer—its fonts, Control Panel, and your printer. In reality, Windows Explorer and Internet Explorer are the same program, with Windows Explorer tailored slightly more for working with local files and folders and Internet Explorer for the Internet.

Starting Windows Explorer

To start Windows Explorer, click the Start button. Then choose Programs and Windows Explorer. The Windows Explorer window appears.

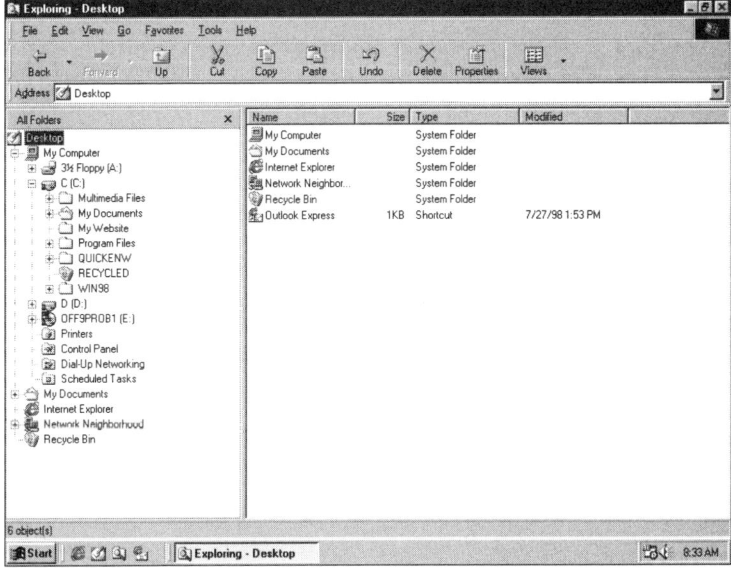

Windows Explorer uses a **folder pane** to show the **folder** structure and a **file pane** to show **subfolders** and the files in the active folder. Windows Explorer provides file information, including the file size in **kilobytes** and the last modification date. (The last modification date is the date someone last fiddled with the file by changing its contents.)

continues

Windows Explorer *(continued)*

Selecting Disks

To select a disk, click the disk icon in the folder pane.

Selecting Folders

To select a folder, scroll through the folder pane until you see the folder you want. Then click the folder.

If the folder is a subfolder in another folder, you may need to first select the parent folder and display its subfolder. You do this by clicking the parent folder.

Windows Explorer alerts you to subfolders

Windows Explorer adds the plus sign (+) to a folder icon if the folder it represents has subfolders.

Selecting Files

To select a file in the active folder, scroll through the file pane until you see the file. Then click it.

You can select more than one file at once by clicking the first file, holding down the Shift key, and then clicking the last file. Or you can hold down the Ctrl key and click each file you want to select.

Opening Files

To open a file in the active folder, scroll through the file pane until you see the application or document. Then double-click the file. When you double-click an application, Windows starts the application. When you double-click a document, Windows starts the application in which the document was created and tells the application to open the document you clicked. For example, when you double-click a document created in Microsoft Word, Windows launches Word and displays the file you selected.

WinZip

WinZip is the name of a popular, easy-to-use compression utility. WinZip, like PKZIP, scrunches files so that they take less time to transmit. You can usually find an evaluation copy of WinZip at any web site that provides **shareware.** For example, you can always find a copy at *http://www.zdnet.com.*

Working Offline SEE Offline

World Wide Web

The World Wide Web (also known as W^3, the Web, and WWW) is a set of multimedia documents that are connected so that you can jump from one document to another by way of hypertext links, usually with a click of a mouse. If this definition sounds complicated, it's probably because I've used a few terms you may not know: document, multimedia, and hypertext. Let me define these terms for you and make the whole picture clear.

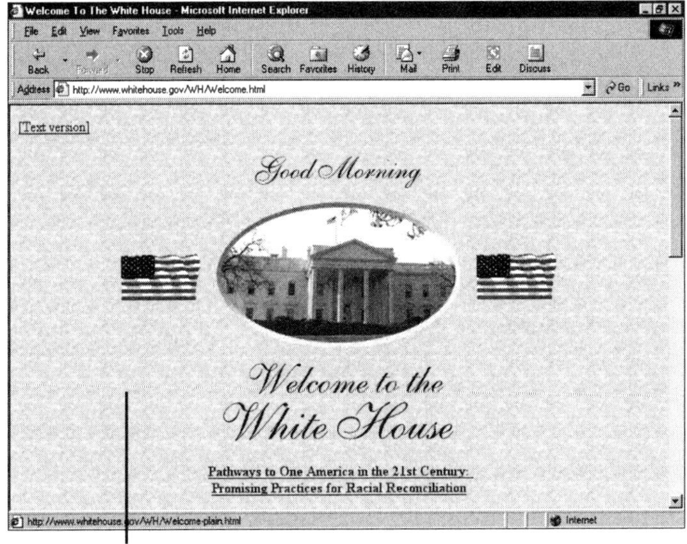

The White House's page on the Web.

Let's start with the key term, *document*. A document is a report that describes something. Often, documents are on paper. In fact, you've probably created hundreds of paper documents: book reports in grade school; thank-you letters to distant, gift-giving relatives; and perhaps lengthy term papers in college. You wrote these documents on paper, but if you had produced and displayed them on a computer screen, they still would have been documents, right? So now you know what I mean by document.

The *multimedia* part relates to the fact that when you create and display a document on a computer, you aren't limited to words. You can place pictures in a document, for example. And you can place sound objects. Just about any object a computer can create, display, or play can be placed in a document. So now you know what I mean by multimedia.

continues

World Wide Web *(continued)*

And now we come to what makes the World Wide Web unique—the *hypertext* part. Hypertext is a connection, oftentimes called a **hyperlink**, that lets you jump from one document to another. Suppose you're reading a document that talks about the U.S. Department of Commerce and what it does. This document references, let's say, the Office of the President with a hypertext connection, or hot link. You click the words "Office of the President" and see a new document that talks about the president.

So to return to the original definition, the World Wide Web is simply a set of multimedia documents that are connected using hypertext links. And by clicking these hyperlinks, you can jump from one document to the next.

Before I finish this discussion, I should make two more points. First of all, to view a World Wide Web document, you need to have a web **browser** such as **Internet Explorer** (the focus of this book) or **Netscape Navigator.** Second, if you're new to the World Wide Web and don't know where to begin, start with the web site *http://www.yahoo.com*. It provides a directory of thousands of different World Wide Web servers.

If you want to get technical about hot links, read this

The documents you read, or view, with a web browser are written using something called **HTML.** In fact, the web browser client uses HTML instructions to display a document on your screen. These HTML instructions also include uniform resource locators, or **URLs.** And when you click a hot link, the web browser client uses the URL and the Hypertext Transfer Protocol, or **HTTP,** to find and display the other document.

WWW SEE **World Wide Web**

XML

XML, or extensible markup language, is a powerful new type of document starting to appear on the **World Wide Web**. The power of XML comes partially from its ability to not only display information but to encode the information with meaning in a way that a computer can understand. This will allow for more useful searches of web pages, as well as programs that can manipulate data within web pages in ways not possible with **HTML**.

XSL

XSL, or extensible stylesheet language, is a companion to XML, allowing XML documents to be formatted in ways that are both more powerful and more elegant than CSS supports.

SEE ALSO **CSS**

Yahoo!

The very popular Yahoo! web site essentially amounts to a directory of Internet web sites and pages. In other words, Yahoo! works much like a table of contents in a book. To use Yahoo!, you first look through the Yahoo! directory's main headings to find an information category. Then you click the category's **hyperlink** to see the subcategories within the category. Then you click the appropriate subcategory's hyperlink to see the sub-subcategories within the subcategory. You continue this process until you get to a web page or web site with the information you want.

One thing to recognize about Yahoo! is that while it's a search service, its fundamental organization differs from that of an index-style search service like **AltaVista.** An index-style search service, in effect, maintains an index of web sites and pages which you access by using a **search engine.** A directory-style search service like Yahoo!, in effect, maintains a table of contents of web sites and pages which you typically use by exploring categories and subcategories of hyperlinks. (Yahoo! does provide a search engine, too, so this isn't precisely true, but it's a pretty accurate generalization.)

ZIP

ZIP actually refers to a data-compression technique. When people say a **file** is zipped, they usually mean it's been compressed using the **PKZIP** or WinZip utility. To use a zipped file, you have to unzip it. If a file has been zipped with PKZIP, for example, you have to unzip it with PKUNZIP.

Troubleshooting

Got a problem? Starting on the next page are solutions to the problems that sometimes plague new users of Internet Explorer 5. You'll be on your way—and safely out of trouble—in no time.

E-Mail

You Don't Know Someone's E-Mail Address

You want to send so-and-so an **e-mail** message, but you don't have their address? Don't feel embarrassed. I think this is probably the most common Internet problem of all. Really. Fortunately, this problem is easy to solve.

Call them and ask

Sounds silly, doesn't it? But this really is the best solution. So go on and do it. You need to get both their **username** and the **domain name.** Once you know these bits of data, you just send your message to:

`username@domainname`

For example, if you wanted to send an e-mail message to me, you would send the message to:

`steve@stephenlnelson.com.`

steve is my username, and *stephenlnelson.com* is the domain name.

Ask them to e-mail you so you can reply

Another easy gambit is to have the person e-mail you. You need to know your e-mail address so you can tell them. But if they can send you an e-mail message, you'll know their e-mail address and be able to reply. You can, for example, click the Reply To Author toolbar button as you're reading their message to display a New Message window, already addressed to the person. Or you can right-click their name in the message window so that Microsoft **Outlook Express** displays a shortcut menu. Choose the Add To Address Book command to tell Outlook Express you want to permanently record the person's e-mail address in your **Address Book.**

Conduct a search using a search engine

If you want to contact a person and don't know their address, telephone number, or even if they have an e-mail address, you can use a search engine to find the person's e-mail address if they have one. Several search engines have "people search" features. All you have to do is display a search engine's home page and see if you can find a hyperlink called "people search" or something similar. Click this hyperlink, and then enter all the information you know about the person in the appropriate boxes. If the search turns up empty, try again with a different search engine.

E-mail the user's postmaster

If for some reason you can't call the person or contact them some other way—maybe a quick letter—you can also try e-mailing a request to the postmaster at the e-mail post office that serves the **host** on which your friend is a user. I'm not really sure this will work, by the way. Sometimes it will; sometimes it won't. What you're really doing is asking for a special favor from the person who administers the e-mail messaging system for the domain. But to do this, you can usually e-mail your message to:

```
postmaster@domainname
```

Of course, this means you need to know the domain name. So you may need to call the organization for that. But let's say you want to e-mail a message to an old school chum. You know he works for Parnell Aerospace in Taiwan, but you don't know his username. You need to call Parnell Aerospace and get the domain name of the Taiwan office—let's pretend it's *parnell.com.tw*. Then you e-mail your request to the following address:

```
postmaster@parnell.com.tw
```

World Wide Web

You Can't Connect to a Web Server

If you can't connect to a web server, either you've got the uniform resource locator (URL) wrong or the web server isn't allowing you to connect—perhaps because it's overworked and cranky. Unfortunately, both problems produce the same symptoms.

Check the URL

Carefully check the URL. The first part of the URL should be *http://*. So make sure you've entered this part right. Note that the slashes are really slashes and not backslashes. The server name will probably look something like this: *www.microsoft.com*. In other words, it usually starts with the acronym *www* and then is followed by the web server owner's **domain name.** So to connect to Microsoft Corporation's web server, you enter *http://www.microsoft.com*. (Of course, if you're connecting to some other company's web server, you don't enter *microsoft*.)

Be patient

Even if you've entered the URL correctly, you still may not be able to connect. If you get a message when you try to connect to a web server that says something like "host not responding" or "host connection failed," it may just be that the web server isn't available or is too busy to respond.

In this situation, your only real recourse is to try later. If the web server is just really busy, by the way, you might be able to connect a few minutes later.

Your Connection Speed Is Slow

Bandwidth is the practical problem of the Internet and especially of the World Wide Web. The problem is that even with a fast modem, downloading web pages with lots of pretty pictures takes time. Add animation or sound to a web page and minutes turn into hours—or so it seems. Fortunately, you can do things on your end to minimize the time you spend waiting.

Do something else while you wait

Perhaps the simplest thing to do is just to do something else. Remember that Windows lets you **multitask.** What this means is that you can write that report that's due tomorrow while you're waiting for a web page to download.

Set up the page for offline browsing

You can set up a page to be downloaded while you're away from your computer. This way it'll already be on your computer when you want to view it. This is called **offline browsing,** and it can save you a lot of time if the pages you want to read are usually busy or take a long time to load.

Add an active channel for the web page

Some web sites support **channels.** When a web site does support channels, you can tell the web site that it should routinely send you updated copies of a web page. To do this, click the Add Active Channel button, which you'll see on web pages that can be turned into active channels.

Differentiating between offline pages and channels

Offline pages and channels can be a little confusing at first, but they're really quite simple conceptually. Consider the following: The traditional way of moving content from a web server to your PC is by clicking a hyperlink or supplying a URL. In other words, you give the instruction to move content from a server to a client. With pages set up for offline browsing, in comparison, you can tell Internet Explorer to automatically issue an instruction to move content from a server to a client. And with channels, the web site (without instruction from you or Internet Explorer) moves content from a server to a client.

View text-only versions of web pages

The textual portion of a web page doesn't actually take very long to download. Or at least that's usually the case. Therefore, if what you're really interested in is a web page's textual information and a web server gives you the option, you can indicate that you want to view text-versions of a web site's pages. To do this, you typically click a hyperlink that's labeled something like "text-only."

Web Page Pictures Look Gritty

Let's say you're viewing web pages, but your pictures look gritty. You can sort of make out what you're supposed to see, but the pictures are nowhere close to being photograph quality. This, you're wondering to yourself, is what everybody is getting so excited about?

Increase the number of colors and the resolution

To view photographic images on your monitor, you need to use a SuperVGA monitor. SuperVGA monitors provide greater resolution and display more colors. And you need to tell Windows to use high resolution and lots of color. You probably have a SuperVGA monitor if you purchased your monitor anytime in the last few years. But there's a good chance that you're not using its high resolution and color capabilities. To make sure you are, follow these steps:

1. Right-click the Windows desktop. Windows displays a shortcut menu of commands related to the **desktop.**
2. Choose the Properties command. Windows displays the Display Properties dialog box.
3. Click the Settings tab.

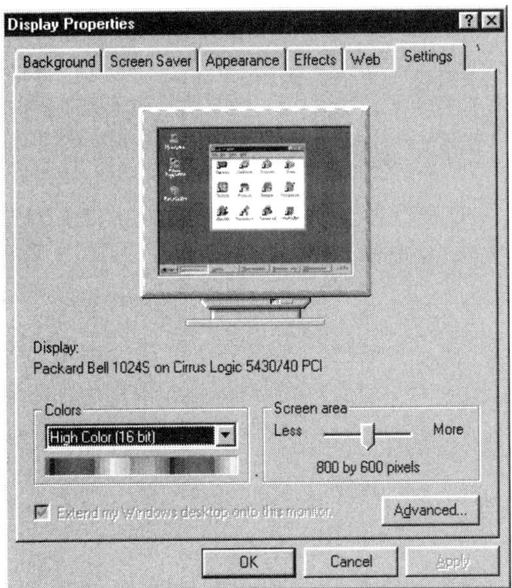

4. If the Colors drop-down list box shows 16 Color, select a higher color setting, such as 256 Color, High Color (16-bit), or True Color (24-bit). The higher the color setting you choose, the more colors you'll see and the better the image quality will be.
5. Move the Screen Area slider to the right to increase the resolution.
6. Click OK. Windows may ask if it can reboot your computer so the display setting changes can take effect. Save any unsaved work, and then go ahead and do this.

Try another web page

Some of the pictures that are used in web pages aren't high-quality photographic images. So if you've verified that you're using a lot of color and a high resolution, view some other web pages. Quite likely, the grittiness you're seeing is in the images themselves and is not the result of a problem with your computer or viewer.

Telnet

You Can't Connect to a Host

If you can't connect to a host using the Telnet service, your problem probably boils down to one of two things: either you've got the uniform resource locator (URL) wrong or the telnet host isn't allowing you to connect. One of these situations you can do something about. The other you can't.

Check the URL

If you get a message when you try to connect to a telnet host that says something like "host unknown," you've got the wrong URL. Plain and simple. So what you need to do is figure out the right URL. Check your source document. Make sure you've entered it exactly as shown. If you did enter it correctly, either your source document is wrong or, just as likely, your source document is out of date.

Be patient

If you get a message when you try to connect to a telnet host that says something like "host not responding" or "host connection failed," it may just be that the telnet host isn't available right now. If you're trying to connect at some really crazy hour (like 3 am) or when the telnet host is really busy (like during prime business hours), the telnet host is quite likely not available.

In this situation, your only real recourse is to try later. If you know what the telnet host's usual hours of operation are and you know that the telnet host is available, you might want to try again in, say, 10 minutes. If you're trying to connect to a telnet host that you don't know much about or you're trying to connect at some crazy hour, it might be best to wait until normal working hours.

You Connect but Can't Log On or Issue Commands

This happened to me just the other day, in fact. I was showing the Internet to a friend. He wanted to telnet to a library in Minnesota. Proudly I typed in the URL. A few seconds later, the host we were trying to connect to responded. It asked for our username and a password. It was weird. I typed these in, successfully logged on, but then couldn't issue any commands. The telnet host told me to type, for example, HELP to get a list of commands. So I typed help, but nothing happened. It told me I could type MENU to get a menu of commands. So I typed menu. Again, nothing.

Pay attention to whether your commands and entries should be uppercase or lowercase

You've probably already figured out what I was doing wrong. The case was important. The telnet host wanted the words HELP and MENU in all uppercase letters. A command name in all lowercase letters like help or menu just wouldn't do the trick.

Actually, as a general comment, I'll also note that anytime you log on to a server running UNIX, the case is relevant. If the server wants all lowercase letters—and that's what it usually wants—you'd better type them. And sometimes, when things are really crazy, the server wants uppercase letters. You had better type them, too.

You Can Issue Commands but You Don't See Them or You See Each Letter Twice

In the previous section, I started to tell you about the embarrassing little episode of telnetting to a library in Minnesota. I have to tell you what happened next. As soon as I figured out the uppercase vs. lowercase business, I could type commands and get the telnet host to do what I wanted it to. But when I typed the command, I wouldn't see it on the command prompt. I would type HELP, for example, but I wouldn't see anything. After I pressed the Enter key, however, I would see a screenful of help information. My friend, I feared, was rapidly losing confidence both in the telnet service and in my abilities as a guide to the Internet.

continues

You Can Issue Commands but You Don't See Them or You See Each Letter Twice *(continued)*

Adjust the local echo setting

What was wrong? The local echo setting. In my case, the telnet client, Windows's Telnet program, needed to have the local echo setting turned on. To do this, choose the Terminal Preferences command. Then select the Local Echo check box.

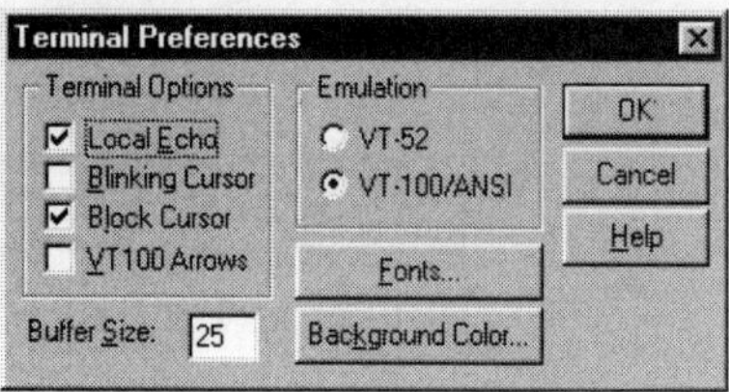

By the way, if you have local echo turned on when it should be turned off, you get double letters for just about everything. Rather than seeing a message like this:

```
Type HELP
```

You see a message like this:

```
TTyyppee HHEELLPP
```

If you get double letters, you should try turning off the local echo setting.

You Can't Disconnect from a Host

Once you've telnetted to a host, you're connected. You need to disconnect from it to get back to the host where you started. Disconnecting isn't difficult. But you do need to know the secret command or escape sequence to disconnect from the host.

Backtrack through the session log

When you initially connected to the host, the host almost certainly told you how to disconnect. Therefore, you may be able to scroll backward and read the stuff you should have read when you first connected. The telnet client, by default, only keeps the last 25 lines or so in its application window. But you may as well try scrolling backward. Click above the Telnet window's scroll bar marker to scroll backward.

Try all the old standbys

To quit whatever you're doing on the host computer, you can probably type an escape character. You might try Ctrl+]. You might also try Ctrl+C.

Quick Reference

Any time you explore a new program, you're bound to see features and tools you can't identify. To be sure you can identify the commands and toolbar buttons you see in Internet Explorer, this Quick Reference describes these items in systematic detail.

Internet Explorer Commands

File Menu

New Displays the New submenu.

- **Window** Opens a new Microsoft Internet Explorer browser window.
- **Message** Opens a new message form so you can write an e-mail message.
- **Post** Opens a new message form so you can post an article to a newsgroup.
- **Contact** Opens the Address Book so you can describe a new contact.
- **Internet Call** Starts Microsoft NetMeeting so you can make an Internet Call.

Open... Displays a dialog box you use to provide the URL of a web page (or other Internet resource) you want to view using Internet Explorer.

Edit With Microsoft FrontPage Opens the current page in FrontPage or FrontPage Express for editing.

Save Saves any changes you've made to the open web page.

Save As... Saves current web page to your hard disk.

Page Setup... Specifies how web pages should be printed.

Print... Prints the current web page.

Send Displays the Send submenu.

- **Page By E-Mail...** Opens a new message form (so you can write an e-mail message) and then attaches a copy of the open web page to the message.
- **Link By E-Mail...** Opens a new message form (so you can write an e-mail message) and then includes the URL for the open web page in the message.
- **Shortcut To Desktop** Creates a shortcut icon that points to the open web page and then places the shortcut icon on your desktop.

Import And Export Imports and exports favorites and cookies to or from other applications.

Properties	Displays a Properties dialog box describing the open web page.
Work Offline	A toggle switch, which if marked, tells Internet Explorer to show cached copies of web pages rather than download and then show new copies of web pages.
Close	Closes the Internet Explorer window.

Edit Menu

Cut	Removes the current selection and places it on the Clipboard so you can paste the selection somewhere else.
Copy	Makes a copy of the current selection and places the copy on the Clipboard so you can paste the selection somewhere else.
Paste	Moves the selection currently stored on the Clipboard to the insertion point.
Select All	Selects all the text in the window.
Find (On This Page)	Searches for specified text on the current web page.

View Menu

Toolbars	Displays the Toolbars submenu.
	Standard Buttons Adds or removes the toolbar of standard buttons. (Internet Explorer also marks the command with a check mark when the buttons are present.)
	Address Bar Adds or removes the URL Address bar from the window. (Internet Explorer marks the command with a check mark when the Address bar is present.)
	Links Adds or removes the Links bar from the window. (Internet Explorer marks the command with a check mark when the Links bar is present.)
	Customize Allows you to add, remove, or rearrange buttons on the toolbar.
Status Bar	Adds or removes a status bar from the window. (Internet Explorer also marks the command with a check mark when the status bar is present.)

continues

View Menu *(continued)*

Explorer Bar	Displays the Explorer bar submenu.	
	Search	Opens the Search bar.
	Favorites	Opens the Favorites bar.
	History	Opens the History bar.
	Folders	Opens the Folder bar.
	Discuss	Opens the Discussion bar if you have Office 2000 installed.
	Tip of the Day	Opens a bar that displays the Tip of the Day.
Go To	Displays a list of recently visited web pages.	
Stop	Tells Internet Explorer to stop whatever it's doing—such as retrieving a web page.	
Refresh	Tells Internet Explorer to read the web page again (from the web server) and then redraw the window.	
Text Size	Displays a list of font sizes you can use to display web page text.	
Encoding	Lets you change the alphabet for the language of the web site.	
Source	Displays the HTML instructions that create the web page.	
Script Debugger	Displays a submenu of commands you can use to debug scripts.	
Full Screen	Uses practically the full screen to show the web page by removing Internet Explorer's menu bar and application window title bar. (To return to the regular screen view, click the Fullscreen toolbar button.)	

Favorites Menu

Add To Favorites...	Adds the current web page location to a list of favorite pages.
Organize Favorites...	Displays the Organize Favorites dialog box, which you can use to reorder, rename, or delete your favorite web pages.

About the other Favorites menu commands

The Favorites menu also lists the favorite pages you've already added by using the Add To Favorites command. To move to one of these pages, choose its menu command.

Tools Menu

Mail & News	Displays the Mail & News submenu.
	Read Mail — Starts your e-mail client (probably Microsoft Outlook Express).
	New Message — Creates a new message in your e-mail client.
	Send A Link... — Creates a new e-mail message with a hyperlink to the current web page.
	Send Page — Creates a new e-mail message with the current web page attached.
	Read News — Opens your news reader (probably Microsoft Outlook Express).
Synchronize	Retrieves updated copies of those web pages you've set up for offline browsing.
Windows Update	Opens the Windows Update web site to download software upgrades.
Internet Option	Displays the Internet Options dialog box so that you can specify how Internet Explorer works.

Help Menu

Contents And Index	Starts the Help program.
Tip of the Day	Opens a bar displaying tips on using Internet Explorer.
For Netscape Users	Opens a web page devoted to Netscape users learning Internet Explorer.
Web Tutorial	Opens the web tutorial web page.
Online Support	Opens Microsoft's online support web page.
Send Feedback	Opens a web page providing ways to give feedback to Microsoft.
Repair...	Automatically fixes problems with the Internet Explorer program.
About Internet Explorer	Displays the About Internet Explorer dialog box and gives the available memory and system resources.

Internet Explorer Toolbar Buttons

Goes back to the previous web page.

Lists the web pages you can move backward to view.

Goes forward to the next web page.

Lists the web pages you can move forward to view.

Tells Internet Explorer to stop whatever it's doing—such as retrieving a web page from some distant web server.

Tells Internet Explorer to read the web page again (from the web server) and then redraw the window.

Opens your web home base, or home page.

Opens your default search engine web page.

Displays the Favorites folder, which lists your favorite web pages.

Displays a history of the web sites and pages you've visited using the Explorer bar.

Displays a menu of commands for reading e-mail, creating new messages, sending web pages or URLs to people via e-mail, and reading newsgroup articles.

Prints the current web page.

Starts FrontPage Express (if you installed the full version of Internet Explorer) so you can edit or view the HTML instructions of the open web page.

Displays the Discuss toolbar (if you have Office 2000), which lets you comment and view other people's comments about the current page or document.

Outlook Express Commands

File

New	Displays the New submenu.	
	Mail Message	Creates a blank e-mail message.
	News Message	Creates a blank newsgroup post.
	Folder	Creates a new folder.
	Contact	Creates a new contact in your Address Book.
Open	Displays contents of the selected folder or e-mail message.	
Save As...	Lets you save the selected message.	
Save Attachments	Displays a submenu listing the selected message's attachments. To save an attachment, choose its submenu command.	
Save As Stationery...	Uses the selected message to create new message stationery.	
Folder	Displays the Folder submenu.	
	New	Creates a new folder.
	Move	Moves the selected folder to a new location.
	Rename...	Renames the selected folder.
	Delete	Deletes the selected folder.
	Compact	Compresses the selected folder so it does not waste space.
	Compact All Folders	Compresses all your folders so they save space.
Import	Displays the Import submenu.	
	Windows Address Book	Imports names and addresses from a Windows Address Book .wab file.
	Other Address Book...	Imports names and addresses from another e-mail client's address book.
	Messages...	Imports messages from another e-mail client.

continues

File Import *(continued)*

	Mail Account Settings...	Imports the mail account settings information used by another e-mail client.
	News Account Settings...	Imports the news account settings information used by another newsreader.
Export	Displays the Export submenu.	
	Address Book...	Exports names and addresses from Outlook Express to another e-mail client's address book.
	Messages...	Exports messages from Outlook Express to another e-mail client.
Print...	Prints selected e-mail message.	
Switch Identity...	Allows you to switch the settings to those for another person who uses Outlook Express.	
Identities	Displays the Identities submenu.	
	Add New Identity...	Creates a new Identity for another user of Outlook Express.
	Manage Identities...	Opens the Manage Identities dialog box to control how Identities are used.
	Logoff User	Logs off the current user so another user can log on.
Properties	Displays or changes properties of selected folder or e-mail message.	
Work Offline	A toggle switch, which if marked, tells Outlook Express to show cached copies of messages and newsgroup articles rather than download and then show new copies of web page.	
Exit	Closes Outlook Express.	

Edit

Copy	Copies the current selection.
Select All	Selects all the folders or e-mail messages shown in the message pane.

Find	Displays the Find submenu.
	Message... Opens the Find Message dialog box to allow you to search for a message.
	Message In This Folder... Finds a message in the selected folder.
	Find Next... Finds the next message with the specified text.
	People... Finds a name in your Address Book or on the Internet.
	Text In This Message... Searches for the specified text in the selected message.
Move To Folder...	Moves the selected message to another folder.
Copy To Folder...	Copies the selected message to another folder.
Delete	Deletes the current selection.
Empty "Deleted Items" Folder	Empties the Deleted Items folder.
Mark As Read	Marks the selected message as one you've read.
Mark As Unread	Unmarks a message you've previously marked as read.
Mark Connection As Read	Marks all messages in the selected conversation or thread as read.
Mark All As Read	Marks all the messages in the selected folder as read.
Flag Message	Marks a message with a flag for easier sorting and finding.
Find People...	Finds a name in your Address Book.
Find Text...	Finds text in the selected item.
Find Message...	Finds a message in the selected folder.

The newsgroup version of the Edit menu

The preceding table lists the commands that appear on the e-mail version of the Edit menu. If you're working with a newsgroup, Outlook adds the Catch Up command, which marks all messages as read.

View

Current View — Displays the Current View submenu, which lets you customize how Outlook Express displays messages in your folders.

Sort By — Displays a submenu with commands and settings that correspond to sort orders and options.

Columns... — Displays a dialog box you use to specify what information you want displayed in the message pane.

Layout... — Displays a dialog box you use to specify how you want the Outlook Express program to look.

Text Size — Displays the Text Size submenu.

- **Largest** — Uses a font that's the next size larger than the "larger" font.
- **Larger** — Uses a font the next size larger than the "medium" font.
- **Medium** — Uses the default font size for text in the window.
- **Smaller** — Uses a font the next size smaller than the "medium" font.
- **Smallest** — Uses a font that's the next size smaller than the "smaller" font.

Encoding — Displays a submenu with commands that correspond to the different languages you can use to view messages.

Previous Message — Displays the last message you viewed.

Next — Displays the Next submenu.

- **Next Message** Displays the next message.
- **Previous Message** Displays the previous message.
- **Next Unread Message** Displays the next unread message.
- **Next Unread Thread** Displays the next unread thread.
- **Next Unread Folder** Displays the next unread folder.

Go To Folder... — Allows you to open another folder.

Expand	Shows the replies to the selected message or article.
Collapse	Hides the replies to the selected message or article.
Stop	Tells Outlook Express to stop whatever it's doing—such as retrieving a message.
Refresh	Tells Outlook Express to read again the messages in a folder or the articles in a newsgroup.

Tools

Send And Receive	Displays a submenu that lists Dial-Up Networking connections you can use to pass e-mail messages to and from the Internet. To send and receive messages, you choose a connection.
Synchronize All	Downloads all items set up for offline viewing.
Address Book...	Displays the Address Book, a list of e-mail addresses.
Add Sender To Address Book	Adds the sender of the selected message to your Address Book.
Message Rules...	Lets you set up rules for processing incoming messages.
Newsgroups...	Displays a list of all available newsgroups.
Accounts...	Lets you specify, change, or view the mail, directory, and newsgroup accounts you use with Outlook Express.
Options...	Changes Outlook Express's appearance and operation.

The newsgroup version of the Tools menu

The preceding table lists the commands that appear on the e-mail version of the Tools menu. If you're working with a newsgroup, Outlook changes some of the command names and adds some special commands specifically for downloading articles, downloading newsgroup lists, and filtering newsgroup articles.

Message

New Message	Opens a new message form so you can create an e-mail message.
New Message Using	Displays a submenu that lists the stationery you can use for e-mail messages. To create a message with a particular stationery, choose the submenu option that corresponds to the stationery.
Reply To Sender	Creates a new message that replies to the sender of the currently displayed message.
Reply To All	Creates a new message that replies to all the recipients of the currently displayed message.
Forward	Sends a copy of the currently displayed message to someone new.
Forward As Attach	Sends a copy of the currently displayed message as an attachment to someone new.
Create Rule From Message...	Creates a message rule based on the selected message.
Block Sender...	Creates a rule preventing messages from the selected sender from being downloaded.
Flag Message	Flags the selected message.
Watch Conversation	Alerts you when a new message is received in the current conversation.
Ignore Conversation	Stops watching the selected conversation.

Help Menu

Contents And Index	Starts the Help program.
Read Me	Displays a small text file with late-breaking information about the Outlook Express program.
Microsoft On The Web	Displays a submenu listing Microsoft web sites and pages you can visit.
About Microsoft Outlook Express	Displays the About Microsoft Outlook Express dialog box and gives the available memory and system resources.

Outlook Express Toolbar Buttons

	Opens a new message form so you can create an e-mail message.
	Displays a submenu that lists the stationery you can use for e-mail messages.
	Creates a new message that replies to the sender of the currently displayed message.
	Creates a new message that replies to all the recipients of the currently displayed message.
	Sends a copy of the currently displayed message to someone new.
	Prints the currently selected message.
	Deletes the selected item.
	Connects Outlook Express to your mail server so Outlook Express can send messages you've created and receive messages other people have sent you.
	Displays a submenu with options you can use when sending or receiving messages.
	Displays your Address Book.
	Searches for a particular message.
	Displays a submenu that lists different options you can use to find messages, text, or people.

Special Characters

A

B

E

F

G

H

I

J

K

L

M

N

O

P

W

X

Y

Z

The manuscript for this book was prepared and submitted to Microsoft Press in electronic form. Text files were prepared using Microsoft Word 97. Pages were composed by Stephen L. Nelson, Inc., using PageMaker 6.5 for Windows, with text in Minion and display type in Univers. Composed pages were delivered to the printer as electronic prepress files.

Cover Designer
Tim Girvin Design, Inc.

Interior Text Designer
Kim Eggleston

Layout / Illustration
Stefan Knorr

Project Editor
Paula Thurman

Writers
Jason Gerend and Steve Nelson

Technical Editor
Jeff Adell

Indexer
Julie Kawabata

Printed on recycled paper stock.